I0834539

1880 CENSUS

DECATUR COUNTY, TENNESSEE

Transcribed by

BYRON SISTLER
BARBARA SISTLER

Janaway Publishing, Inc.
Santa Maria, California
2012

1880 Census Decatur County, Tennessee

Originally published, Nashville, 1993

Reprinted by:

Janaway Publishing, Inc.
732 Kelsey Ct.
Santa Maria, California 93454
(805) 925-1038
www.JanawayGenealogy.com

2012

ISBN: 978-1-59641-114-2

Made in the United States of America

INTRODUCTION

The entries are arranged alphabetically by head of household. In general an entry comprises all members of a given household in the order they appear on the original schedules; any individuals whose surname differed from that of the household head are shown as a separate unit.

An asterisk (*) identifies each entry which does not consist of an entire household.

The symbol (B) identifies black or mulatto individuals or families. If the (B) follows the first name in the entry it means the entire household is black. Where the household is mixed, each black person is separately identified with the (B).

The symbol (I) was supposed to identify Indians, but actually was used by the enumerators to represent various racial mixtures.

The number after each name stands for the person's age. An entry reading <1 means a child under one year of age. The number in parentheses at the end of the entry indicates the stamped page number on the original schedules. Since the stamped number appears on every other page, the page following the numbered one assumes the same number.

It should be remembered that the 1880 census schedules included information not previously required. Of primary interest to the genealogist is the data concerning relationship of each member of the household to the household head--wife, son, grandson, etc. Also of great importance is the fact birthplace of not only the individual but of each of his parents was included. This information is not shown on this transcription; consequently the researcher should make every effort to examine, or have someone examine, the original schedules.

Sistlers

Nashville, TN
February 1993

AARON, Thomas N.? 42, John T. 11, Absolom W. 9, James F. 6, Rosa T. 8, Samuel F. 2 (12)
ADAIR, H. E. 38 (f), M. J. 32 (f), L. F. 28 (f), S. A. 26 (f), M. U.? 19 (f), Margrett 12, F. L. 9 (f) (78)
ADAIR, J. D. 33 (m), M. B. 27 (f), M. P. 5 (m), W. J. 1/12 (m) (78)
ADAIR, W. G. 36 (m), M. C. 33 (f), E. A. 4 (f), A. J. 2 (f) (78)
ADAMS, James 27* (30)
ADAMS, John R. 29*, Jessie 20, Oliver P. 2, Elmer P. 3/12 (26)
ADKERSON, Absolom L. 25*, Tennessee B. 18 (11)
ADKERSON, Thomas L. 18, Manerva A. 21 (11)
ADKISSON, Ellender 84* (12)
ADKISSON, I. Samuel 34, Mary 34, William A. 13, Nancy E. 10, Mary 8, James E. 5, John A. 3 (15)
AGNEW, J. P. K. 34 (m), Salina A. 26, Jane Bell 8, Lena C.? J. 4 (87)
AGNEW, Wm. R. 57, Narsissa L. 55 (87)
AKEN, John F. 42*, Leantine L. 32, James E. 11, Lizza M. 9, Carrie V. 7, Thomas W. 5 (26)
AKIN, James 43?*, Huda? 43 (90)
AKIN, Mariah 35 (B), Millard W. 17, William R. 12, Abram 10, Albert 2, Eliza 14 (30)
AKIN, Monro? M. 28*, Mollie 27, Calvin 8, Bular 7, James 5, Cora 2 (90)
AKIN, William R. 51*, Elizabeth 42, William J. 22, Tennessee 17, John H. 10, Allice F. 10, Allison 7, Robert J. 50, Susan T. 38 (29)
AKIN, Winnie 60* (89)
ALFORD, William B. 40, Martha 28, Jasper N. 7, Columbus A. 1 (32)
ALLEN, R. P. 61 (m)*, Nancy 21 (79)
ALLISON, A. B. 29 (m), Alsa 38 (20)
ALSTON, Charles A. 28, Margret A. 21, Jessee P. 3/12 (57)
ALSTON, Martha C. 59*, Carrie 17 (56)
ALTOM, Joseph H. 38*, Eliza A. 32, Lucy A. 17, Mary J. 15, William J. 14, Louisa A. 13, Rebecca E. 11, John B. 8, Thomas L. 1 (28)
ANDERSON, Anza? 45 (f)James, Margrett? 16, Miles 9 (91)
ANDERSON, George 32*, Eliza 28, Hattie F. 10, Nanie 7, Cracus? 5, Jesse N. 3 (f) (54)
ANDERSON, J. W. 40 (m), S. A. 50 (f), S. A. 19 (f), Andrew H. 18, Sammy T. 17, K. L. 15 (f), May A. 13, A. J. 11 (m), J. W. 8 (m), J. A. 6 (f) (60)
ANDERSON, W. A. 26 (m)*, A. B. 25 (f) (82)
ANDERSON, William 20* (57)
ANDREWS, Artis? 3 (f)*, J. C. 8 (m), M. P. 6 (m), S. J. 4 (f), J. H. 1 (m) (74)
ANDREWS, Josey 8*, Cora 5 (42)
ANDREWS, Pompy 76* (B), Chasty 39 (f), Arch 16, King 14, Wesly 12, Jo 7, Sylvester 2 (40)
ANGLIN, Cornelius 53, Rebeca A. 37, Permelian 30, John T. 19, Sarah P. 14, James M. 5, Flurina B. 4, Mary E. 2 (4)
ANGLIN, Henery A. 28, Martha A. 20 (4)
ANGLIN, Joseph S. 24, Martha J. 20, Molly A. 1 (4)
ANGLIN, Nancy 60, Manerva C. 30, James W. 7, Angeline 3 (14)
ANGLIN, Richard A. 26, Patsy C. 20 (12)
ANGLIN, William 60*, Phebe 65 (5)
ANGLIN, Willis B. 25*, Lucinda E. 29 (2)
ARMSTRONG, A. 18 (f)* (72)

ARMSTRONG, John 28*, Eliza 22, Nancy J. 4, Lueller 3/12 (90)
ARMSTRONG, Wm. 28, Bettie 21 (86)
ARNETT, Peter 34, Serena B. 30 (59)
ARNOLD, E. E. 16 (f)* (B) (60)
ARNOLD, E. E. 28 (m)*, M. E. 28 (f), M. A. 4 (f), O. M. 2 (f), J. E. 10/12 (m) (75)
ARNOLD, E. J. 30 (m), Mary S. 23 (60)
ARNOLD, J. 20 (m)* (B) (60)
ARNOLD, J. 28 (m) (B), S. 25 (f), J. 6 (m), S. 3 (f) (70)
ARNOLD, James H. 27, Rebecca R. 23 (38)
ARNOLD, L. A. 51 (f), W. M. 22 (m), M. J. 20 (m), A. L. 19 (f), M. J. 16 (f), Emma 14 (69)
ARNOLD, S. 60 (f)* (B), C. A. 10 (m) (69)
ARNOLD, T. P. 39 (m), A. E. 34 (f), Fredonia 10, E. J. 9 (f), D. B. 8 (f), J. E. 7 (m), M. E. 6 (f), L. E. 5 (m), Emma 3, Zetta 1 (69)
ASHCRAFT, Isam 56 (B), Martha 43 (49)
ASHCRAFT, Joel L. 70*, Serelda L. 55 (23)
ASHCRAFT, W. 25 (m) (B), Jane 22, William 2, M. M. A. 5/12 (f) (80)
ASHCRAFT, William 39, Eliza 26, William 17, Malvina 16, Thomas J. 12, John W. 10, Joel C. 8, Dorah 2, Dolla 2/12 (24)
ASHCROFT, Sam 77 (B), Mary 64 (46)
ASHCROFT, Winnie 29* (B), Granvill 5 (46)
ATKINSON, Auriel? N. 37 (m)*, Barbra E. 20, Nancy A. 13, James D. 11, Jose T. 8 (f), Mary E. 5 (26)
ATKINSON, William 35, Mary E. 25, Martha E. 11, William I.? 9, Samuel S. 7 (26)
AUSTIN, Charles W. 22, Eliza A. 18, Lester 1 (1)
AUSTIN, George W. 36, Lydia A. 36, Cintha E. 13, Mary A. 8, Willie A. 6 (f), Robert L. 3 (2)
AUSTIN, James C. 46, Elizabeth A. 45, Ginnie E. 21, Mary J. 19, Lurena A. 14, Salina 12, John M. W. 10, James C. 6 (3)
AUSTIN, James F. 24, Martha A. 18, Leonard L. 2, Adar C. 10/12 (6)
AUSTIN, James M. 48, Charity 44, Jonathan C. 22, Sary A. 19, Henry A. 14, Martha L. 6, Cintha M. 5, Jephtha M. S. 1 (2)
AUSTIN, Timothy M. 8* (3)
AUSTIN, William 36*, Mary J. 44 (15)
AUTRY, J. H. 22 (m), L. 32 (f) (67)
AVERETT, John 58, Mary J. 39, J. E. 15 (f), Mahalia A. 12, Blossom 10 (f), Geo. W. 8, Elijah 6, Philip M. 4, Saml. M. 1 (51)
AYDLETT, Andrew 56* (31)
AYDLUTT, James F. 26*, Anna C. 18, Otto H. 1/12 (57)
BAGSBY, J. L. 41 (m), M. F. 38 (f), R. C. 13 (f), W. G. R. 12 (m), C. J. 8 (f), Lula B. 6, John A. 4, Jas. T. 3 (46)
BAILEY, C. 19 (m)* (68)
BAILY, J. 25 (m)* (68)
BAKER, B. F. 36 (m), Margaret 30, Lilly V. 10, Charles A. 8, Wm. A. 6, John M. 4, Frora E. 2 (92)
BAKER, B. G. 62 (m)*, C. B. 57 (f), R. C. 17 (f), H. E. 15 (f) (64)
BAKER, Geo. 21* (64)
BAKER, J. K. 30? (m)*, Pl E. 29 (f), G. L. 9 (m), V. E. 7 (f), D. E. 6? (m) (64)
BAKER, James E. 32, Dolly 25, Elbert W. 2, Minnie B. 9/12 (89)

BAKER, Thos. H. 59, Alletha 58, Larken 18, Charles 16, Josie 32, G. P. 22 (m) (89)
BAKER, Thos. W. 24 (89)
BAKER, W. E. 25 (m)*, T. E. 23 (f), E. C. 3 (m), O. C. 1 (m) (64)
BAKER, Wm. 29, Mildred 29, Laura E. 7, Mary A. 5, Vinson 4, Eddie D. 2 (89)
BALCUM, John C. 26, Elenor J. 23, Meranda 7, Arra 4, Minny 1, James W. 25 (40)
BALEY, G. W. 21 (m), R. A. 16 (f) (66)
BALEY, J. H. 35 (m)*, Mary L. 42, Warren 11/12 (19)
BALEY, Lee 54 (f), M. J. 19? (f), A. C. 15 (f) (66)
BALINGER, Aaron 69*, Fanny D. 40, Perry 22 (92)
BALINGER, John 45, Mary 43, Wm. A. 22, Mary A. 17, Eliza A. 15, Beedie 12, Caroline 7 (92)
BALLARD, C. Ann 40, Elizabeth 14, William 12, John 7, George 6, Maggie 2 (53)
BARBER, Allen L. 54, Winney 54, Permelia C. 27, William A. 21, James H. 18, Mahalia L. 15 (13)
BARBER, John T. 26, Elvira E. 22, Annah F. 1 (14)
BARBER, Wm. 20* (52)
BARKER, E. 72 (m), L. A. 54 (f), Wortte? 22 (m), A. J. 20 (m), F. B. 18 (m), D. 12 (m), M. L. 30 (f), V. A. L. 28 (f) (83)
BARKER, W. E. 27 (m), Dorinda 23, John 6, M. J. 2 (f), W. A. 1/12 (m) (83)
BARKOFSY, Olli O. 31 (m)* (58)
BARNETT, Catharine 50 (34)
BARNETT, G. 30 (m) (B), Ellen 35 (80)
BARNETT, J. 60 (f)*, M. J. 34 (f), W. L. 29 (m), M. R. 19 (f) (76)
BARNETT, Jeff P. 35, Pricilla C. 29, W. Virgil 10, E. Jane 8, M. Joannah 5, M. Esther 3, N. G. Gaston 1 (43)
BARNETT, John 24, Amanda 22, Mary 2 (53)
BARNETT, John 57*, Elizabeth 41 (42)
BARNETT, Wm. L. 27* (56)
BARRENGER?, Hannah 35* (92)
BARTHOLOMEW, G. W. 31 (m), Melvina 25, Julia F. 5, Joseph M. 3, G. W. 1 (m) (47)
BATEMAN, R. M. 41 (m), M. M. 39 (f), W. 10 (m), J. M. 8 (m), T. P. 1 (m), E. 70 (f) (77)
BATES, R. L. 37 (m)*, E. A. 34 (f), G. P. 12 (m), D. B. 6 (f) (75)
BAUCUM, A. 33 (m), Mary Bell 28, Dora 8, Dewit 2 (89)
BAUCUM, Geo. F. 30*, Permela 28, Robert D. 6, C. V. 4 (f), Eliza A. 2 (91)
BAUCUM, James 27, Sarah B. 20, Miles L. 7/12 (90)
BAUCUM, Mary 53, Martha 19, Wm. 17 (89)
BAWCUM, C. N. 22 (m)*, F. L. 23 (f) (63)
BAWCUM, George 41*, Altha L. 68 (89)
BAWCUM, Linda 38*, Mary Bell 6 (51)
BEASLEY, N. 12 (f)* (65)
BELCHER, M. A. 50 (f)*, W. 24 (m), T. J. 22 (m) (74)
BELL, J. M. 28 (m)*, Calie F. 18 (87)
BELL, James R. 35* (2)
BELL, John 45* (B) (37)
BELL, Silver 46 (B), Benjamin 23, John 18, Ella C. 16, Martha D. 14, Eddie 7 (15)
BENNETT, W. A. 48 (m)*, E. C. 37 (f), E. P. M. 17 (m) (74)
BENNETT, W. Jassee 29, S. R. 25 (f), M. J. 4 (f), Jno. W. 2, M. L. 10/12 (m), J. M. 22 (m) (46)

BENTHAL, Mark 20, Luvina B. 17 (41)
BERKS, Mary 19* (38)
BERRY, Matilda 76 (B) (28)
BIDLOCK, Amanda M. 60* (36)
BINGHAM, Charles A. 37*, Elizabeth 31, Samuel U. 4, Deborah A. C. 2, Artemus L. 1/12 (27)
BINGHAM, Emily 9* (15)
BINGHAM, Ike 51 (B), Martha 37, Fannie 11, James 7, William 3, Nimrod 2 (27)
BINGHAM, Leondus 40, Julia F. 35, Robert L. 10, Mary E. 10, Emily 9, Louisa 6, Leantine 5, James E. 2 (10)
BINKLEY, A. 65 (m), T. A.? 14 (f) (67)
BIRD, Joseph T. 26*, Elizabeth 21 (12)
BIRD, Quire? 38 (f)* (48)
BIRNBAUM, Ermina 17*, John L. 12 (6)
BISHOP, Esq.? 65, Mary Ann 30, W. Harvy 7 (85)
BISHOP, Green 26, Vintha 26?, Calvin 5, Oscar 3, Thomas 1 (89)
BISHOP, Tempa 32* (92)
BLACK, John 23, Rosa 17 (35)
BLACK, John B. 46, Nancy C. 44, William J. 21, Martha E. 13, Mary J. 11 (37)
BLACKBERN?, Henry 25, Martha A. E. 34, Laura E. 7, Mary E. 5, Louis M. 2 (6)
BLACKBURN, A. J. 36 (m), M. J. 30 (f), E. J. 8 (f), J. B. 4 (f), W. J. 2 (m) (49)
BLACKBURN, James 53, Sarah 47, Saml. 30, M. J. 29 (f), J. F.? 22 (m), Margret 20, Thos. 18, S. E. 16 (f), J. A. 15 (m), Lucinda 11, J. P. 10 (m) (49)
BLACKBURN, Jane 67, N. J. 35 (f), G. W. 23 (m), Sarah E. 18 (19)
BLACKBURN, Martha 28*, S. A. 9 (f), N. J. 7 (f), A. E. 1 (f) (50)
BLACKSTOCK, Thos. 21* (50)
BLAKE, William H. 41, Gracie L. 29 (11)
BLAKELY, John 26 (55)
BLAKELY, Leantine 4* (55)
BLOUNT, Jas. R. 12* (44)
BLOUNT, John H. 16*, H. C. 14 (m), Fannie 12, Laura 11, Milard 9, J. D. 8 (m) (44)
BOATWRIGHT, Martha 75* (53)
BOGAN, Abram 50* (B), Eliza 43, Abram 20, Lee 17, John 15, Mary 12, William 11, Adaline 6, Eddy 5 (28)
BOGAN, Almeda 11* (16)
BOGAN, Elizabeth 18* (22)
BOGAN, George W. 25, Aida L. 20 (27)
BOGAN, Henry 27* (B), Anna 20, Solomon 1 (28)
BOGAN, Levi 60 (B), Mandy 40, Frances 18, Lurrsa 17, William J. 15, Leander 14, Tennie F. 14, Isaac P.? 4, Zilpha P. 6, Anderson 1 (3)
BOGAN, William 53*, Sarah 52, Benjamin R. 23, William R. 17, Newton J. 13, Thomas 13 (27)
BOGUM?, Rufus 15* (B) (23)
BOHANNAN, B. C. 27 (m), E. A. D. 28 (f), ____ 10 (f), E. E. 9 (f), J. H. 6 (m), J. C. 3 (m), T. J. 1 (m) (67)
BOHANNAN, J. H. 55 (m), M. A. 53 (f), M. A. 14 (f), J. H. 2 (m) (63)
BOHANNAN, L. Y. 25 (m), Marthy 19 (63)
BOHANNAN, S. T. 21 (m), C. 20 (f) (63)

BOHANNAN, T. J. 24 (m)*, J. A. 25 (f), C. B. 2 (m) (63)
BOLEN, William B. 75*, Susannah E. 65 (17)
BOMAN, Geo. 50, L. 46 (f), H. 20 (f), T. 18 (m), E. 16 (f), S. L. 13 (f), W. N. 12 (m), S. J. 8 (f) (70)
BOMAN, H. 36 (m)*, M. C. 29 (f), S. H.? 12 (f), J. A. M. 8 (m), M. J. E. 5 (f), T.? H. H. 3 (m), W. P. 1 (m) (66)
BOMAN, Mary 58*, G. C. 28 (m), S. H. 22 (m) (63)
BOMAN, W. D. 30 (m)*, S. J. 29 (f), S. A. 6 (f), B. A. 4 (f), Dixie 3 (m) (63)
BOMAN, Wm. 36, M. E. 25 (f), T. H. 12 (m), J. W. 8 (m), S. O. 7 (f), S. L. 5 (m), D. L. 2 (f) (65)
BOMON, J. W. 44 (m)*, Eliza 38, Johnithan 12, Robert 10, Sidney 6, Laura 5, Lonzo 1 (60)
BOODIE, Henry 33, Martha 40, Chales 12, Mary 10, Sarah 8, Willie 6, John 4, Green 2 (93)
BOODIE, John 36, Martha 32 (91)
BOODIE, Mariah 37* (91)
BOODY, William 29* (B), Sarah 22, _____ 1/12 (f) (61)
BOONE, Mary A. 43*, Wm. J. 17 (47)
BOSTIC, E. D. 47 (m), J. E. 38? (f), C. 16 (m), C. L. 14 (f), J. C. 12 (m) (66)
BOTTON, J. 41 (m)*, M. A. E. 39 (f), J. H. 19 (m), J. R. 15 (m), J. E. 12 (f), J. F. 10 (f), N. J. 8 (f), J. C. 7 (m), M. F. 5 (f), A. H. A. 2 (f) (67)
BOTTON, W. F. 27 (m), M. A. 22 (f), E. A. 2 (m), J. H. 11/12 (m) (67)
BOUKENNEDY?, V. S. 5 (f)* (74)
BOURLAND, Asa L. 18 (3)
BOWLUND?, William 56*, Mary 52 (43)
BOX, J. 54 (m)*, F.? 44 (f), S. 23 (f), J. H. 22 (m), S. 18 (f), J. 15? (f), R. 8 (f), S. 6 (m), M. E. 2 (f) (Jr.) 3/12? (m) (71)
BOX, James 24*, Martha 17 (90)
BOX, Mary 55, H. 18 (m), G. 15 (m), T. 24 (m), J. 20 (m) (71)
BOX, R. 25 (m), S. 24 (f), M. 2 (f), A. 1 (f) (71)
BOX, S. 15 (m)* (72)
BOX, T. 24 (m)* (72)
BOYD, F. B. 57 (m), Eliza J. 54, Eliza W. 24, W. P. 17 (m), J. F. 15 (m), A. S. 12 (m) (93)
BOYD, Fenton S. 49*, Mary A. 48 (56)
BOYER, Richard 28, Viola 28, John 6, Marietta 3, Dorah 1/12 (34)
BOYER, Zerilda 58, Janie 36 (34)
BRADLEY, Isham 58 (B), Mersca 36, Monroe 21, Isham jr. 19, Mathew 17, Dona 16, Samuel 12, Eller 10, Allen 8, James 6, Fanny 3 (35)
BRADLY, Ed 23 (87)
BRADLY, John 27, Josie 21, Moriah 22, Becie 7, Alas 5 (f) (87)
BRAKEN, J. C. 8 (m)* (74)
BRANCH, Frank 12* (85)
BRANCH, Joseph 60, Bicy 50 (f), James 16, Martin 13 (85)
BRANCH, Pollie 50*, Dick 28, John 20, Fredonie 18 (86)
BRANDON, Chrona? 45 (m), Fila A. 41, Lora B. 13, Sallie E. 8, Elixander M. 6 (91)
BRANDON, William 47, Martha A. 39, John W. 22, George H. 17, Albert A. 15, Charley Y. 9, Walker W. 9 (35)
BRASHEAR, Isaac E. 55*, Ethalinda 52, Geo. W. 8, Ora E. 6 (52)
BRASHEAR, Isaac T. 33*, Solomon 19 (30)
BRASHEAR, Jesse W. 46*, Marth B. 36, David W. 16, Joel E. 13, Walter 11, Ora 8, P.

Logan 5, Minnie 2, Deler M. 1 (f) (52)
BRASHEAR, Martin 23*, Elizabeth J. 26 (27)
BRASHEAR, Philip R. 53*, Ora B. 32, Willie A. 12, Walter J. 9 (57)
BRASHEAR, Samuel 42*, Sarah F. 32 (29)
BRASHEAR, Thomas 85 (B), Leah 90 (27)
BRASHEAR, William 26*, Riley 19 (27)
BRASHEAR, Zedakiah 65* (29)
BRASHEARS, Jenny 51 (B), J. A. 14 (m) (50)
BRASHER, Eveline 40* (12)
BRASHER, Isaac 28*, Ellen 27, John 5, Willie 4, George 2, Emma 8/12, William 25, Riley 20, Eliza 38, Mary A. 34 (11)
BRASHER, Jefferson P. 34, Sary A. 37, Eliza J. 15, William S. 12, Nancy L. 10, James A. 9, Mary C. 7, Lucy A. 5, John 2, unnamed 2/12 (m) (11)
BRASHER, John 54*, Kizzie 53, Viana 19, Phillip R. 20, Elentine 14, Linentine 14, Rebeca A. 13 (12)
BRASHER, John E. 24, Sary E. 18, Oliver 5/12 (12)
BRASHER, Joseph S. 35, Amand C. 35, Eliza E. 8, Cora E. 5 (12)
BRASHER, Martin V. 31*, Malinda C. 28, William R. 10, Mary E. 7, Cora E. 4, Perry H. 1 (11)
BRASHER, William R. 29*, Sarah E. 29, John A. 10, James M. 7, William W. 5, Mary L. 2, Nancy 70 (13)
BRASHER, thomas 30 (B), Creasey A. 28, John T. 12, Martha A. E. 5, Josephene 4, Adar T. 2, James W. 7/12 (10)
BRAWLEY, Nancy M. 56, Octava E. 27, Gustave? L. 21, Will T. 18, Byron E. 10 (f), Bulah B. 5, John W. 1 (19)
BRAWLEY, T. G. sr. 57 (m)*, Caroline 54, P. Caroline 21, F. Marion 18, Arba 14, Andrew 1 (51)
BRAWLEY, Thomas G. J. 25*, Martha J. 19 (56)
BRAWLEY, William F. 27, Cintha C. 28, Mary E. 6, Cordilla E. 2 (7)
BRAY, F. J. 25 (m), S. E. 24 (f), Maud M. 1 (62)
BRAY, John 27*, Lamira 23, William 5, Thomas 1 (56)
BRAY, W. Parker 47*, Elizabeth 46 (56)
BRAZILL, Sysntha M. 68, Eliza A. 28, Martin J. 1 (36)
BREVARD, B. F. 38 (m)*, Ann B. 36, A. A. 19 (m), Wm. A. 17, L. E. 15 (m), F. J. 11 (m), James Q.? 10, Elvus 5, _____ 7/12 (f) (87)
BREWER, H. 50 (m), S. 38 (f), M. J. 21 (f), S. 17 (f), M. M. 15 (f), C. 13 (f), S. A. 10 (f), J. J. 8 (m), B. A. 3 (f) (68)
BREWER, J. 45 (m), M. 33 (f), E. J. 14 (f), E. H.? 12 (f), L. A. 8 (f), J. H. 6 (m), W. D. 4 (m), C. F. 1 (m) (68)
BREWER, Mat 22* (39)
BRIANT, David S. 37, Sarah A. 22, M. K. M. 5/12 (f) (54)
BRICE, J. T.? 30 (m), E. E. 25 (f), S. P. 9 (m), M. 7 (f), E. L. 4 (f), S. 3 (m), A. A. 11/12 (f) (72)
BRIGANCE, Edward S. 19, Josephus 17, Martha A. 41 (3)
BRIGANCE, John H. 55*, R. C.? 55 (f), P. H. 23 (m), Laura J. 21 (52)
BRIGANCE, William S. C. 23, Mary F. 16, Leonard L. 1, Martha J. 17 (3)
BRIGHT, Geo. W. 46, Mahalia 31, Jas. A. 7, Arba A. 5, John M.? 3, George W. 1/12 (52)
BRIGHT, Mary H. 46* (45)

BRIGHT, Sarah C. 74* (33)
BRISANTINE, Charles 7*, Albert 4 (54)
BRITT, George W. 28, Amanda E. 26, Nancy E. 7, Frances I.M. 5/12 (32)
BRITT, Henery J. 27, Nancy J. 33, Hugor F. 7, Henery W. 5, Robert Lee 2, Mary M. 7/12 (14)
BRITT, William M. 27, Sarah 20, Mary L. 5, Martha J. 3, Mora 1 (14)
BROCK, James 25, Margarett 23, Melvin W. 3, James W. 2, Christopher C. 3/ (22)
BROCK, John 19, Mary 22, Cordelia 1 (22)
BROCK, Mary 43*, Emily G. 16 (19)
BROCK, Tilman 50, Martha 25, Frances J. 10 (59)
BROWN, Abner 54, Malinda 21, James 11, Nancy Jane 3, Mary A. 20/30 (22)
BROWN, J. M. 21 (m)* (72)
BROWN, Jackson 38*, Eliza T. 43, John H. 13, Malinda F. 12, Laura T. 12, Bensam L. 9, Ellen D. 7 (5)
BROWN, Julia A. 65, William G. 45 (33)
BROWN, M. 32 (m), M. 24 (f), W. T. 8 (m), S. J. 7 (f), J. A. 4 (m), J. H. 3 (m), L. 3/12 (f) (75)
BROWN, R. 28 (m)*, M. 31 (f), L. 10/12 (f) (71)
BRUCE, A. 9 (m)* (87)
BRUCE, W. M. 17 (m)* (66)
BRYANT, Bettie 18* (8)
BRYANT, Jas. H. 37 (49)
BUCKANNAN, Francis 33*, Almerine 22, Calvin E. 6/12 (27)
BUCKER, William J. 24 (15)
BUCKINGHAM, Andy 53* (B), Hariett 53, Henry 16 (23)
BUCKINGHAM, E. E. 17 (f)* (65)
BUCKNER, E. 48 (m), M. L. 45 (f), W. A.? 16 (m), M. F. 11 (f), O. E. 10 (m), L. G. 7 (m), J. I. 5 (m), S. J. 2 (m) (82)
BUNCH, C. 24 (f) (B), L. A. F. 5 (f), L. B. 8/12 (f) (81)
BUNCH, Clem 23 (B), Puss 23 (31)
BUNCH, John 75*, M. 68 (f) (75)
BUNCUM, Wm. 65*, Parlee 52 (93)
BURGER, Julia 12* (7)
BURKETT, D. M. 24 (m)* (65)
BURKETT, M. N. 26 (m), R. C. 28 (f), M. E. 3 (f), A. E. 2 (f), E. G. 4/12 (m) (69)
BURNES, Wm. 28* (90)
BURNS, J. B. 35 (m)*, Mary 35, Flora 3 (44)
BURNS, P. 21 (m), Hannah 21 (86)
BURRELL, Wm. 18* (B) (61)
BURRUS?, Jehu 35*, Frank 38, Larania R. 13, N. A. 11 (m), Mahaly E. 8, Sallie A. 6, Alla U. 5, John A. 5/12 (89)
BURTON, Cora 11* (56)
BURTON, M. 34 (f), C. L. 12 (f), J. D.? 10 (f), T. 8 (m), S. 5 (m), E. 2 (m), M. J. 8/12 (f) (74)
BURTON, Manuel 17* (B) (54)
BURTON, S. 77 (f)*, S. S. 34 (m) (74)
BURTON, W. C. 34 (m)*, A. J. 28 (f), F. 5 (f), E. 3 (f), J. 8/12 (m) (75)
BUSBY, Mary E. 6* (7)

BUSSELL, C. C. 39 (m)*, M. A. 35 (f) (74)
BUSSELL, Gus 16* (B) (30)
BUSSELL, J. 53 (m)*, A. 56 (f), J. J. 27 (m), M. 25 (f), John 23, F. A. 18 (f) (75)
BUSSELL, Judah 72 (f)* (74)
BUSSELL, S. 41 (m)*, S. 32 (f), Juda 14 (f), M. 13 (f), S. F. 11 (f), E. J. 9 (f), W. 4 (m) (76)
BUSSELL, William H. 30*, Mary 27, Cora 2 (56)
BUTLER, Christopher 24*, Sarah 23, Mary 4, Eicea? 1 (m) (11)
BUTLER, Christopher C. 25*, Sarah A. 22, Mary T. 4, Edgar E. 1 (17)
BUTLER, James M. 67*, Amanda 52, Mandrid V. 18, Manda V. 18 (17)
BUTLER, John 35, Ellen 14, Noah 12, John T. 8, Robert L. 3 (23)
BUTLER, Thomas A. 43, Clementine 23, Mary F. 17, William W. 13, Sary D. 11, James J. 8, Hariet A. 6, Allice J. 2, John M. 11/12 (11)
BUTLER, Viola 26*, Virginia C. 10, William 6, James 4 (24)
BUTLER, William W. 26, Ebert E. 1, Allice A. 5/12 (4)
CACY, Ransom 56* (B), Minerva 32, Simeon 19, Dr. Kiley 15, Maberry 13 (29)
CADE, G. B. 21 (m)* (94)
CADE, John 18* (B) (27)
CADE, John 33, Berrilla 28, Alace P. 7, Edna L. 6, Flora B. 4, Charley L. 3, Willis 6/12 (58)
CADE, Levi D. 52*, Hannah E. 54, Ida Belle 16 (21)
CAGLE, B. 34 (m), M. A. 35 (f), J. D. 12 (m), A.? J. 11 (f), S. E. 6 (f), J. A. 5 (f), W. R. 1/12 (m) (72)
CAGLE, D. 59 (m), E. 55 (f), S. 24 (f), N. 21 (f), J. D. 8 (m) (68)
CAGLE, H. C. 51 (m), C. J. 38 (f), Samuel 15, C. J. 14 (f), W. M. 12 (m), M. E. 8 (f) (65)
CAGLE, I.? 40 (m), M. M. 43 (f), E. C. 21 (f), M. A. 15 (f), W. J. 12 (m), J. N. 10 (m), N. M. 8 (f), J. W. 2 (m), C. 1 (m) (68)
CAGLE, Marthy 19* (62)
CAGLE, Mary 16* (90)
CAGLE, T. C. 37 (m), E. E. 17 (m), J. G. 14 (m), M. C. 11 (f), M. S. 8 (f) (65)
CAIN, Ellen 38* (90)
CAISY, B. F. 28 (m), M. A. 24 (f), N. M. 3 (f), ____ 1 (f) (67)
CALNICK?, N. W. 26 (m), M. E. 24 (f), L. E. 2 (f), M. E. 18 (f) (62)
CALVIN, Calvin C. 41, Fanny S. 18, Emer C. 16, Robert H. 13, Nancy D. 11, John F. C. 8, Jacob H. 5, Mary E. 1 (39)
CAMP, Rachel 63*, Permelia F. 39 (29)
CAMPBELL, C. 32 (m)*, M. J. 32 (f), John 6, M. T. 3 (f) (78)
CAMPBELL, David 26 (B), Eliza 28, Cora? 6, Preston 4, Willie 2, Harriett 55, Neely 23 (f), Julia 15 (27)
CAMPBELL, Peter 22 (B), Jose? 21 (f), Maggie 2, Victoria 5 (27)
CAMPBELL, Presley 52 (B), Charlotte 50, Daniel 23, Martha 20, Mary 18, Eliza 16, Fannie 14, Dela 10, Catharine 5 (27)
CAMPBELL, R. P. 32 (m), E. C. 24 (f), M. E. 7 (f), J. S. 4 (f), B. A. 2 (m) (64)
CAMPBELL, W. W. 34 (m), M. J. 38 (f), J. F. 9 (f), W. L. 2 (m) (65)
CANTREL, Poley 29 (m)*, Mary 24, Sam T. 3, Estes W. 2 (90)
CARLTON, Julius O. 26, Mary L.? 20 (57)
CARROLL, Eliza 56, Martha 38, J. L. 29 (m) (46)
CARROLL, Fifer 20* (B) (28)
CARTER, harrison W. 10* (7)
CARY, Benjamin 27 (B), Tennie 22 (29)

CARY, Patsy 55* (B), Ester 30 (27)
CARY, Sarah C. 43, William P. 20, Emily 19, Ledona 12, George F. 10 (25)
CASEY, Houston 22 (B), Kizza 20, Ella 6/12, Alba 24 (9)
CASEY, John L. 61, Mary 45 (6)
CASEY, Matt 16* (B), Willie 8 (15)
CASEY, Sirus 34* (B), Ann 34, Ransom 6, George 3, Nancy M. E. 2 (15)
CAUDEL, Anderson C. 24, Martha A. 23, John A. 1 (14)
CAUDEL, David G. 53*, Martha T. J. 43, Shadrach A. 19, Cintha J. 15, David W.? V. 13, Lucinda C. 12, Martha J. 4, William A. 2, Andrew T. 8/12 (6)
CAUDEL, Elizabeth 55 (15)
CAUDEL, Jefferson F. 24, Robert J. R. 23, David S. 10/12 (6)
CAUDEL, Jonathan S. 22 (6)
CAUDEL, William J. 22*, Mary P. 23, Dora C. 1 (14)
CAUDLE, Marion F. 18*, Louisa 26 (12)
CAUDLE, Martha J. 18* (14)
CAUDLE, Mary L. 16* (14)
CENTHAL, Meriah 47*, Clinton M. 22 (36)
CHAINEY, L. 68 (m)*, M. 73 (f), A. E. 32 (f) (70)
CHALK, James 49*, Mary 36, J. H. 12 (m), Estil 10 (f), Effa 14/365, Etta 14/365 (50)
CHALK, Wm. H. 24, D. M. 23 (f), J. A. 4 (m), Ola 10/12, Ida 10/12 (48)
CHANEY, O. P. 30 (m), M. J. 30 (f) (60)
CHERRY, Charls 26, Eliza P. 16, Elmer 2/12 (87)
CHESTER, Martha 51, Nancy 28, Rebecca 22, Emma J. 17 (42)
CHESTER, William 4* (42)
CHILDERS, Sarah A. 60, Angelkine 27, Morris 20, Elizabeth 18, Taylor B. 2 (91)
CHILDERS, Wm. 37, Cintha 26, James R. 6, Ratiy? 3 (f) (91)
CHOAT, Andrew 55* (B), Mahalia 50, William 4 (21)
CHOAT, More 28* (B), Easter 25, Randle 19, Clay 15, Mat 10 (20)
CHRISTENBERRY, George 42*, Eliza 33, Fredonia 17, Gooch 10, Ona L. 1 (57)
CHURCHWELL, Indiana 44* (22)
CHURCHWELL, John 23, Mary 30, Alice 4, Comfort 45 (f) (49)
CHURCHWELL, Jos. 24 (B), Lu 21 (f) (24)
CHURCHWELL, M. J. 25? (f)* (49)
CHURCHWELL, Mathew 47 (B), Richard 21, Ellen 19, Andrew 17, Nars? 15 (m), Isam 12, Nelson 9, Mary 8, Osker 5, Mathew 8/12, William 8/12 (28)
CHURCHWELL, Richard C. 66*, Emeline 46 (6)
CLARKSON, C. C. 13 (m)* (76)
CLAY, E. 37 (m) (B), M. C. 26 (f), S. P. P. 7 (f), B. F. 5 (m), J. H. 3 (m), M. I. P. 6/12 (f) (76)
CLENNEY, Alva H. 55, Susanah 52, Eliza Ann 21, Joseph H. 19, Robert M. 15, Samuel L. 13, Henery W. 9 (1)
CLENNEY, Ben 64* (51)
CLENNEY, Benj. M. 31, Lucinda 30, Luana R. 7, Vesta H. 5, William A. 3, Arteler A. 8/12 (1)
CLENNEY, James M. 33, Mancy J. 24, Alsa A. 4, Cintha A. 2, Martha E. 1 (1)
CLENNEY, Jesse A. 26, Mary E. 21, Eddie L. 3, Charle M. 9/12 (1)
CLENNEY, William 29, Sary A. 28, Alva W. 7, Mary S. 4, Bertha J.? 1 (1)
CLIFFT, J. W. 48 (m), Dianna 46, W. R. 17 (m), J. F. 16 (m), E. E. 14 (m), Sister 12, C. G. 7

(m), G. W. 4 (m) (62)
CLINSHER?, James W. 21*, William H. 17 (31)
COATS, J. E. 19 (m)* (75)
COATS, M. 18 (f)* (70)
COATS, M. E. 51 (f), Wm. G. 24, J. K. 20 (f), L. E. L. 18 (f), M. P. 14 (f), R. C. 8 (m) (46)
COBB, Benjamin F. 29, Harriett C. 27, Mary E. 7, Sopphira J. 5, Celina A. 3, Gilbert S. 8/12 (26)
COBLE, J. L. 52 (m), Elizabeth A. 45, N. J. 21 (f), B. P. 18 (f), Wm. H. 18, G. H.? 15 (m), J. O. 13 (m), L. E. 11 (f), A. J. 8 (m), E. W. 6 (m), J. W. 26 (m) (87)
CODA, Jesse L. 27*, Mary 66, Margaret A. 22 (15)
CODY, Ransom L. 39*, Nancy A. 39, Mary C. 10, William M. 8, Adaline 3, Amanda E. 3/12 (33)
COGGINS, E. C. 23 (f)* (82)
COGGINS, J. J. 32 (m), M. P. 30 (f), M. E. 4 (f), L. C. 1 (f) (82)
COLE, C. 46 (m), M. A. S. 21 (f), J. R. 19 (m), W. C. 17 (m), C. A. 15 (m), T. L. 12 (m), M. E. 9 (m) (77)
COLE, Christeen 40* (92)
COLE, J. R. 18 (m)* (79)
COLE, Jane 38*, Mary 19, Merit? 15 (f), George 13, Huldy 10, James 8 (89)
COLE, M. A. 66 (f), F. 34 (f), L. A. 2 (f) (67)
COLE, Sally 52* (60)
COLEMAN, Manerva 65*, Luiza 1/12 (90)
COLLENS, M. J. 10 (f)*, J. A. 6 (m) (60)
COLLENS, Ry 52 (f) (B), M. S. 19 (f), L. F. 17 (f), J. H. 14 (m), Anny 1, W. W. 1/12 (m) (62)
COLLENS, S. D. 25 (m), M. L. B. 23 (f) (60)
COLLET, J. W. 44 (m), J. G. 18 (m), M. E. 8 (f) (63)
COLLET, R. A.? 6 (f)* (70)
CONDOR, C. 42 (f)*, William 12 (79)
CONDOR, C. 45 (f)*, W. 13 (m) (76)
CONDOR, C. 73 (f)* (74)
CONDOR, J. 30 (f), Sarah 13, S. H. 2 (m) (79)
CONDOR, J. 40 (f), Sarah 14, S. H. 3 (m) (84)
CONDOR, Jane 42, E. 18 (f), D. 14 (m), Juda 11 (f), J. 6 (f), Jinne 4, P. S. 1 (m), S. 22 (f), J. 3 (m) (76)
CONDOR, W. 24 (m)* (75)
CONRAD, G. E. 56 (m), E. B. 48 (f), M. N. 22 (f), W. P. 21 (m), Elie 19, Jo 17 (m), Marthy 14, B. 13 (m), Alen 11, A. A. 9 (f), A. 6 (m) (65)
CONRAD, J. J. 56 (m)*, W. S. 50 (m), P. M. 45 (m), C. 58 (f) (65)
CONWAY, Elinor 12* (B) (28)
CONWICK, S. 25 (f)* (69)
COOPER, Green 25 (B), Margarett 25, Joseph 4, John 3, Green 1 (30)
COOPER, Joseph 37, Rebecca A. 35, Frank C. 3, Jacob 1 (41)
CORBIN, Alexandria 26 (m), Fannie 18, John 4/12 (27)
COTHAN?, W. J. 32 (m)*, Dela A. 19, Mamie E. 2, Bessie 1 (85)
COUNTIS?, John 38*, Minerva 36, Samuel 12, Mary 10, Margurete 7, John 5, Dick 1 (34)
COVINGTON, W. R. 31 (m)*, M. E. 22 (f), W. I. 4 (m), M. E. 2 (f) (83)
COX, Hugh 37*, Catherine 35, John R. 7, Hugh A. 5, Elmore 3, Flora H. 11/12 (91)

COX, J. R. 33 (m), Mary C. 17 (f), Lonzo 11, Willie 6 (86)
COX, James 25*, Martha 22, Walter S. 11/12 (90)
COX, Wm. 10?, Parthena 32, Mary 29, Phinas 11 (88)
COX, Wm. 34, Sarah 24, Mollie 3 (90)
CRAIG, Aggie 70 (B), Mariah 35 (4)
CRAIG, Clabon 52 (B), Willie 18, Lizzie 12, Mary 18, Lina 10, Cintha J. 8 (4)
CRAIG, Melvin 25 (B) (27)
CRAL, Cally? 67, Liza 24, Ada 6 (66)
CRAWLEY, Diannah 22*, George 5, Laura 3, Robert 6/12 (23)
CRAWLEY, James? M. 36*, Laura 17, Lilly 1, Thomas D. 37 (23)
CRAWLEY, L. D. 64 (m)*, Mary J. 58, May 28, Richard Y. 21 (23)
CRAWLEY, Michell 22, Amanda 20, Flora 10/12 (24)
CRAWLEY, William 67*, Margarett 67 (24)
CREASY, Adam 39, Elizabeth 49, Samuel 26, William R. 18, George 16, Lavisa 13 (32)
CREASY, Bird S. 31, Nancy K. 28, Mary E. 10, Elizabeth J. 8, Rebeca J. 6, Cora E. 2, Virgina V. 8/12 (10)
CREASY, Caleb N. 43*, Sarah C. 35, Lucinda A. 13, William G. 10, Sarah J. 6, Julia E. 4, Mary C. 1 (32)
CREASY, Elijah 27, Vina 37, Ephraim V. 9/12 (32)
CREASY, George 30*, Nancy E. 25, Cora E. 5, Dorah F. 3, Columbus W. 1 (32)
CREASY, Henery T. 24, Mancy J. 19, Mary F. 8/12, Mary G. 64 (8)
CREASY, Jeremiah M. 49, Susan M. 38, John W. 20, James R. 16, Lucinda J. 13, Mary E. 10, Benjamin H. 5, Mahala P.? 2 (32)
CREASY, Nancy F. 33*, Cora R. 4 (32)
CREASY, Sina M. 44* (32)
CREASY, Stephen F. 69, Matilda J. 52, Lucy E. 21, Albert Y. 18, Allice Grant 15. Margarett S. 12, James P. 6 (32)
CREASY, William H. 20* (32)
CREASY?, Bird F. 23, Maranda E. 28, Laura D. 3, Ally E. 2/12 (f) (31)
CREDGINGTON, Robt. 25*, Nancy 38, Lyda 31 (21)
CREWS, Wm. 14* (62)
CRIDER, Joseph 24, Jane 47, Ida 16 (57)
CROOK, F. 16 (m)* (B) (79)
CROOK, T. 17 (m)* (B) (76)
CROWDER, C. H. 28 (m), Martha J. 19, Ellie M. 9/12 (90)
CROWDER, J. A. 52 (m)*, S. E. 54 (f), L. M. 26 (f), J. L. 21 (m) (75)
CRUSE, Cintha 30*, Hetta 7 (89)
CRUSE, Malinda 55*, Emeline 21, George 19, Granville 16, Mahally 13 (89)
CULP, Phillip 59 (B), Ama 69, Malird 21 (f), Phillip 18, James 11, Ida 7, Isabelle 10/12 (10)
CULVER, Thos. 29, N. 28 (f) (69)
CUNEY, J. 19 (m)* (80)
CUNNINGHAM, Riley 27*, Alace 24, Eller M. 4, Minni O. 7/12 (55)
CURLEY, John 24* (2)
CURREY, G. K. 49 (m), M. A. 39 (f), L. E. 15 (f), J. H. 14 (m), J. R. 12 (m), J. F. 11 (m), J. M. 6 (m) (83)
CURRIN, J. W. 25 (m)*, Margret 23, M. F. 4 (f), A. C. 1 (f) (50)
CURRIN, W. D. 52 (m)*, Tennessee 48, John H. 28, M. E. 24 (f), L. A. 19 (f), Charles 13, Marion 10, E. A. 2 (f) (50)

CURRY, G. W. 27 (m), M. E. 24 (f), A. B. 5 (m), J. P. 3 (m), J. J. 4/12 (m) (64)
CURRY, Jas. H. 69, Elender 75, N. J. 36 (f) (48)
CURTIS, Chaton? 19 (m)*, Mary 20 (92)
DABBS, Ellen 30 (B), Bill 5, Roy 3 (35)
DARLING, Narcissus 38, Malina E. 35 (7)
DAVIS, Andrew 21 (B), Creacy 21, James 4, Anderson 1, William H. 3/12, Eliza 40 (21)
DAVIS, Ann 30* (B), Abram 10, Henry 8, Ed 6, Frank 5, Allice B. 2/12 (23)
DAVIS, G. B. 23 (m), E. S. 22 (f), W. F. 1 (m) (49)
DAVIS, George W. 21*, Frances E. 20, Ida M. 1 (13)
DAVIS, Green B. 66, Jemima 57, Nicey R. 32, Sary A. 30, Martha J. 27, Cintha A. 25, Mary A. 21, Margaret S. 19, Emily Lee 16 (4)
DAVIS, J. Asberry 31*, Penelope 29, Wm. A. 2, T. L. 2/12 (m) (46)
DAVIS, James A. 45, Menerva 36, Joseph W. 13, Sarah J. 10, Benjamin 8 (34)
DAVIS, James P. 19* (38)
DAVIS, John A. 24, Kizar A. 22 (f), James D. 4, John W. 1 (13)
DAVIS, John V. 24, Mary 26 (4)
DAVIS, John W. 19* (39)
DAVIS, Joseph 26* (14)
DAVIS, L. Frank 46, M. E. 44 (f), Cora 10 (49)
DAVIS, Layfatte 25* (5)
DAVIS, Maranda 51, Mary J. 31, Martin L. 10 (13)
DAVIS, Mary 58* (5)
DAVIS, Monroe 21* (B) (27)
DAVIS, Nathan C. 26*, Allice 33, Benjamin F. 7, Edgar H. 2, Mary Ella 5/12 (25)
DAVIS, Robert D. 51, Rilda 31, Lafayette 10, Ellen 6, William C. 4, Nancy E. 3, Lucinda J. 2, Lucy A. 4/12 (29)
DAVY, Brad 20* (B) (21)
DAVY, Peter 32* (B), Elizabeth 24, Mary 5, Lola E. 4, John 1 (30)
DE COLEY?, Agnes 27, C. R. 4 (f), Daisey P. 7/12 (45)
DEAN, Thomas 27, Susan 28, Cora 4, George 5/12 (54)
DEES, E. Leonard 30, M. E. 30 (f) (47)
DEES, Green 66, Caroline 50, M. A. 20 (f), R. T. 13 (m), Elenora 11 (45)
DEFOE, Willie 21*, Bettie 24 (29)
DELANIE, N. C. 45 (f)* (83)
DELARY?, Nancy E. 27*, John D. 4, Martha A. 2, Isaac A. 24/30 (24)
DENISON, Curry P.? 40*, Nancy J. 35, Kitty 15, William R. 13, Mary A. 12, Granvil L. 10, Rosetta 7, Bertha 3/12 (56)
DENISON, F. W. 11 (m)* (45)
DENMON?, W. D. 5 (m)*, S. C. 4/12 (m) (78)
DENVER, H. P. 36 (m), Callie 25, _____ 1/12 (f) (86)
DEPREST, Abe 20* (B) (85)
DERUSSETT, Polly A. 70, Jane 50, Jno. W. 6 (49)
DETON, Boss 24 (B), Cass 23 (36)
DEVYHOUSE, Cordela 17* (41)
DIAL, Andrew J. 47, Sarah 48, William 19, Madison 13, Iteba? 12 (f), Isaac 8, Estella 4 (26)
DIAL, Colvin 48, Mary A. 46, Maggie 14, Nancy 11, Thomas 7 (25)
DIAL, James M. 22, Margarett E. 22, Andrew D. 3, Sarah E. 3/12 (26)
DIAL, Samuel 24, Martha A. 20, Nary A. 4 (f), William H. 3/12 (26)

DICKERSON, A. E. 17 (m)* (63)
DICKERSON, S. E. 46 (f) (63)
DICKEY, T. D. 28 (m), E. 35 (f) (64)
DICKSON, Abraham T. 77, Louisa J. 58 (3)
DICKSON, Charles H. 35*, Winney 36, Henery G. 7, Martha L. 4, Isaac H. 5/12 (1)
DICKSON, Ellen 17 (B) (11)
DICKSON, William 24, Lear 30, Calvin 10, Martha 8, John 6, Rabe 4, Mary 2 (50)
DICUS, John 30*, Mary R. 23, Rhoda M. 21, Fannie E. 11, Mary A. 7 (21)
DICUS, Ose 29, Sarah S. 27 (21)
DIXON, Charity 70* (B) (57)
DIXON, Charley 24* (B) (56)
DIXON, Frank 14* (B) (59)
DIXON, Isabell 46 (B), Mary 21, Lewis 20, Elic 16 (m), Barnard 13, Tenny 10, Thomas 7 (35)
DIXON, John 40 (B), Mira 45, Sarah 17, Cora 14, Dora 7, Betty 5, Anna 2 (43)
DOBBS, Ann E. 19 (47)
DOGUE, James M. 45, Mary C. 40, Martha E. 19, Alvira 16, William J. 15, Samuel L. 13, Jasper N. 11, Ider L. 9, Dorah 6 (40)
DOHERTY, Fonton 24* (89)
DOHERTY, J. G. 31 (m), R. L. 21 (f), Ida 5, Ada 5, R. 2 (f) (62)
DOHERTY, James 13* (58)
DOHERTY, James W. 49* (58)
DOHURTY, George 22 (89)
DOIL, I. J. 27 (m), F. A. 23 (f), P. C. 2 (m), J. C. 1 (m) (61)
DOIL, J. R. 28 (m), P. A. 28 (f), C. A. 3 (m), Clona A. 2, Flora 10/12 (61)
DOIL, J. W. 20 (m), V. R. 15 (f) (63)
DOIL, John 71, P. A. 38 (f) (61)
DOIL, W. P. 40 (m), Marthy 39?, E. C. 15 (f), S. B. 12 (f), W. T. 10 (m), J. W. 8 (m), S. J. 6 (m), T. B. 4 (f), L. E. 2 (f), Omega 2/12 (62)
DONAHOO, Thomas 27*, Hillie? 31 (f) (21)
DOOD, E. G. 36 (f), A. M. 13 (m), A. W. 3 (m), O. B. 2 (m), S. C. 8/12 (m), S. M. 27 (f) (67)
DOTSON, A. 15 (m)* (B) (64)
DOTSON, A. 52 (m) (B), P. 62 (f) (76)
DOTSON, A. J. 52 (m), E. A. 39 (f), C. T. 21 (m), B. T. 17 (m), M. E. J. 13? (f), S. E. 8 (f), A. M. A. 5 (f), M. L. 2 (f) (65)
DOTSON, J. 21 (m) (B) (79)
DOTSON, Mary T. M. 35* (15)
DOTSON, W. B. 26 (m), L. Y. 19 (f), A. S.? 14 (m) (60)
DOUGHTEN, Frank M. 30, Permela J. 28, Mary E. 3, Wm. P. 1 (52)
DOUGLAS, H. 35 (m), M. J. 32 (f), M. B. 13 (f), N. P. 11 (f), J. H. 10 (m), W. M. 8 (m), J. M. 6 (m), R. B. 5 (f), E. G. 2 (m) (65)
DOUGLASS, E. 40 (f) (73)
DOUGLASS, J. J. 34 (m)*, R. F.? 20 (f), M. A. 9 (f), J. W. P. 6 (m) (80)
DOWDEN, Sallie A.? 31*, Mollie 28 (51)
DOWDY, Margarett D. 17* (20)
DOWDY, Sarah 42*, John W. 12, Eliza 14 (26)
DOWDY, Wm. 46*, Dilla 46, J. M. 23 (m), Visa 16, B. 14 (m), J. 13 (m), S. 11 (f) (67)

DOWNEY, M. E. 12 (f)* (50)
DOWNEY, Melissa 40* (57)
DRISKELL, Mary A. 45 (41)
DUCK, Francis L. 24, Elizabeth J. 26, Rosa 2, Curry 5/12 (32)
DUCK, Jonathan 41, Sintha C. 38, William B. S. 14, John H. 10 (2)
DUCK, Martha 19* (9)
DUCK, William S. 52, Sarah A. 47, John F. 22, Jonathan H. 19, Allen H. 17, Sary L. 14, William S. 9, Daniel M. 6, Christiana 49 (5)
DUKE, Blackwell 20* (34)
DUKE, J. 16 (f)*, P. A. 6/12 (m) (78)
DUKE, J. 24 (m)* (71)
DUKES, J. A. 25 (m), N. 20 (f), J. A. jr. 2 (m) (71)
DUKES, N. J. 42 (m), M. E. 29 (f), L. B. 11 (f), A. E. 5 (f) (80)
DUKES, W. B. 81 (m), N. 78 (f), M. A. 59 (f), L. A. 46 (f), J. C. 21 (m), J. M. 19 (m), A. J. 17 (m), M. E. 16 (f), M. J. 16 (f) (80)
DUNAVANT, James 26, Vicy 25, W. H. 5 (m), M. O. 3 (f), N. C. 1 (f) (49)
DUNCAN, Bell C. 29 (m), Hannah 37, Eliza E. 8, James M. 15, Amanda C. 12 (26)
DUNCAN, John T. 25, Margarett P.? 19, James M. 1 (26)
DUNCLE, John 24, Margaret G. 17 (17)
DUNKLE, George 17* (54)
DUNN, Harmon 25, Mary C. 21, V. E. 3 (f) (43)
DUNN, Hiram 55, Alice W. 12, Hiram M. 10, Aurther C. 6, Elijah F. 4 (43)
DUNN, J. T. 24 (m)* (45)
DUNN, James 2* (50)
DUNNAVANT, J. A. 24 (m), Sarah 21, S. A. 2 (f), Wm. T. 3/12 (50)
DUNNAVANT, W. Arch 53, S. A. 45 (f), C. H. 21 (m), A. J. 18 (m), E. F. 16 (m), M. E. 13 (f), Samuel 10, M. W. 7 (m), R. A. 5 (m) (47)
DURBIN, Willis M. 50?, Aloi 40, Amand J. 14?, Mary L. 8, John M. 6, Allifor 3, Ida C. 10/12 (22)
DURKEN, Jessee R. 42*, Judea C. 42, Lewis M. 21, Ann V. 16, Robert L. 12, Mary A. 4, William H. 1 (5)
DYAL, Albert H. 20*, Angeline 23, Susan E. 2, Andrew J. 4/12, David H. 4/12 (10)
DYAL, Martin A. 25, Allice W. 28, Walter D. 3 (10)
EARLS, Jefferson F. 14*, Rebeca C. 9, William A. 7, Lucina 5, Frances E. B. 1 (5)
EASLEY, W. 23 (m)* (B), Jane 23, Carry 5 (f), Colonel 3, Sisly 1 (64)
EASON, Jonathan D. 39*, Kiza 38, Frances C. 17, Mary A. 15, Lucinda B. 12 (3)
EASON, Robert 28* (13)
EASON, Stephen 63 (3)
EASON, Theophulus A. 34, Semantha J. 33, Stephen M. 11, John D.? 10, Luana J. 8, Olivari? 7 (f) (3)
EATON, Elizabeth 60* (50)
EDGING, J. B. 22 (m), Fredonia 18 (51)
EDMISTON, Thos. F. 29*, ida T. 22, Alma S. 4, Ann M. 8/12 (21)
EDSWARDS, Lewis C. 53, Margarett E. 17, Amanda C. 15 (16)
EDWARDS, Elentine 7* (13)
EDWARDS, Eliza J. 13*, Sary C. 10 (11)
EDWARDS, George W. 33, Josephene 30, Nannie 3, Willie 1 (29)
EDWARDS, J. W. 38 (m), Martha 39, Mary 14, Anner A. 12, Jos. A. 8, S. W. 5 (m), Warren

3 (19)
EDWARDS, Sarah E. 8* (21)
ELKIN, George W. 55, Mary P. 34 (39)
ELLIOT, Lizzy 22*, Jack 2 (53)
ELLIOT, Mildred 45, Elisha 20, N. Jane 18, Mira? 16, Ruben 10, W. H. 8 (m) (50)
ELLIOTT, T. 74 (m)* (67)
ELVINGTON, A. 34 (m), M. B. 26 (f), W. W. 6 (m), L. M. 4 (f) (75)
EMERSON, Riley 48 (B), Phebe 36, Heneretta 15, Emma 13, Martha 12, George 15, Phillip 11 (15)
ENGLAND, Amon M. 24, Margaret 22, William F. 4, Rebeca 1 (9)
ENGLAND, James A. 29, Mary 24, Ellen J. 2/365 (56)
EPERSON, Richard 38, Martha 36, Ugene 21, Molly 18, thomas 16, Idel 12 (f), William 10, Dorah 8, James 6 (38)
EPPERSON, John 25 (m)* (74)
EPPERSON, P.? 38 (f), A. R. 30 (f), A. Y.? 26 (m), Bell 14, J. P. 7 (m), Jooma? 2 (77)
EPPERSON, R. T. 49 (f)*, T. 14 (m) (74)
ERVIN, Janus? 63, Anna 61, David 17 (48)
ESARY, Louisa 31*, Columbus M. 20, Carnley? 17 (f), Jasper N. 16, Paralee 13, Riley 9, Charles N. 12, Sarah Jane 10, James A. 1/12 (31)
ESSARY, Charles M. 25, Mary E. 25, Calvin L. 5, Greenbery 3, Sary J. C. 6/12 (7)
ESSARY, Christofer C. 23, Camly J. 19, George M. 3/12, Sary P. 13, Riley M. 10 (7)
ESTES, Thomas 58, Arminta 38, Marth D.? 12, George 11, Susan D. 8, Thusa 6, Columbus? 5, Adar 3, Ider 1 (91)
EVANS, E. 18 (m)* (81)
EVANS, E. 21 (m)* (80)
EVANS, J. 24 (m)*, G. A. 21 (f), N. L. 5 (f), M. A. 2 (f) (68)
EVANS, John H. 30*, Ella 23, Thomas H. 2 (53)
EVANS, Nick 45*, S. 31 (f), S. J. 2 (f), J. 9/12 (m) (72)
EVANS, W. R. 27 (m), M. 22 (f), C. A. 3 (f), M. E. 3/12 (f), A. J. 23 (m) (69)
FAGG, James C. 24* (23)
FANNING, Alfred 41, Sarah A. 32, Penelope E. A. 13, William C. 8, John H. 8, Malinda A. 4, Alfred W. 10/12 (12)
FARLOW, James 30 (87)
FARLOW, John 25* (87)
FAULKER, F. M. 21 (m), Jane 24, Lena 1 (86)
FAULKNER, John A. 31, Lee Ann 27, Minzie 9?, Mary A. 4/12 (86)
FAYETT, Willey 20* (45)
FERGURSON, Mollie 15*, Blackwell 20 (43)
FERGUSON, Preston 62*, Nancy A. 58, Mary S. 40, Julia A. 34, Nancy J. 26, Harriett 15 (36)
FERGUSON, William L. 34, Virginia A. 24, Ernest E. 2, Oscer? 1 (29)
FINCH, Catharine 22*, Almanza W. 6, Newton B. 1 (38)
FINCH, Eliza E. 51, Bryant 30, Margret 25, Sidney F. 18, T. Frances 18 (47)
FINCH, Sidney 18* (43)
FINCH, William 49, Margurite 51, Rebeca 24, John 21, Isaac 15, Rutha 9, Robert 9, Cora 1 (39)
FINDLY, Eliza E. V. 45 (37)
FISHER, Andrew 43, Mary 37, Finis 15, Olover 13, Ann 8, Drzilla 7? (36)

FISHER, Arnold A. 49, Mary E. 37, Laury A. 21, Neal S. 20, Joseph S. 15, Elisabeth 14, Leora 9, Sylvanis 6, Thomas 4, Delmer 11/12 (39)
FISHER, Barrett 51 (B), Dona 37, Thomas W. 18, Dora 14, William 13, Ann 10, Daniel 8, Eliza 7, Isaac 6, Belle 2 (16)
FISHER, Bettie 15* (B) (28)
FISHER, Charles W.? 45, Sobrina A. 42, James M. 18, John P. 17, Sofrona A. 15, William F. 9, Charles 6 (35)
FISHER, Danl. H. 30*, Sousan E. 38, Mary E. 6, Troy W. 2, Charles H. 2/12 (39)
FISHER, Emeline 48*, James W. 18 (39)
FISHER, George B. 38*, Lucinda 40 (39)
FISHER, Henry 53 (B), Mary 40, Margarett 13, James 8, Granville 4 (21)
FISHER, Isham 17* (B) (42)
FISHER, Isham 43 (B), Isabel 41, Florence 20, Henry 18, Jane 14, Adaline 11, John 8, Mary 5, Eller 1 (42)
FISHER, J. A. C. 26 (m)*, M. G. 26 (f), L. C. 3 (f), A. B. 1 (f) (81)
FISHER, J. F. C. 31, Effa 17, Sophia 2, Jacob F. 6/12 (35)
FISHER, J. H. 40 (m), M. 30 (f), Wm. 12, Hawkins 7, N. A. 6 (f), Jonathan 1 (49)
FISHER, Jacob F. 65, Elmena 25 (35)
FISHER, Jas. M. 47*, Martha J. 37, Jas. F. 17, Jno. H. 15, Mary E. 14, Nancy J. 21, Martha F. 10, L. A. 8 (f), M. F. 6 (f), E. C. 4 (f), Wm. W. 4/12 (52)
FISHER, John W. 63, Nancy G. 59, Mary F. 20, Martha J. 18 (37)
FISHER, Lafayett 30, Florence G. 24, Elenora 9, Emily C. 7, Martin G. 4, Paul H. 3, Anna K. 9/12 (42)
FISHER, M. B. 44 (m), Mary F. 42, Mary B. 24 (88)
FISHER, M. P. 26 (m)*, H. E. 18 (f), A. H. 1 (m) (77)
FISHER, Mary A. 52*, Newton 18 (39)
FISHER, Matisan 33, Martha A. 26, Elmer 3 (39)
FISHER, Milton B. 35, Tennessee 32, Geneva N. 8, Henry L. 6, Bedferd F. 4, Elvy 2 (37)
FISHER, Paul H. 58*, Ann K. 50, Robert Y. 12 (43)
FISHER, Sam 23*, Wade 20, _____ 25 (f) (74)
FISHER, Thos. F. 20*, Mina 22 (88)
FISHER, William H. 48, Hetty 43, Jenny 7 (B), John 5 (B) (37)
FISHER, William R. 29, Mary D. 36, Ida L. 8, Franklin 3 (39)
FLIPPO, Martha 21*, Mary J. 3, James H. 2, William A. 3/12 (21)
FLOID, G. R. 18 (m)* (64)
FLOWERS, Callie 21* (86)
FLOWERS, G. W. 40 (m), N. 38 (f), K.? E. 17 (f), Luta 14, M. J. 12 (f), J. W. 10 (m), J. J. 8 (m), M. A. 4 (f), infant 1 (f) (78)
FLOWERS, H. 44 (m)*, M. C. 36 (f), H. T. 12 (m), M. E. J. 9 (f), J. W. 7 (m), S. L. 3 (f), S. A. 1/12 (f) (80)
FLOWERS, K.? 63 (f)* (82)
FLOWERS, M. W. 26 (m)*, Malisse 30, V. T. 2 (f), M. A. 10 (f) (81)
FLOWERS?, L. 30 (f)* (78)
FLOYD, Jackson 56?, Elizabeth 57, George R. 19, Martin 12, James 11, Benjamin 10 (85)
FLOYD, Thomas 17*, Mollie 16 (90)
FLOYD, Wm. 22?, Pollie 35, Scott 10, Sheridan 8, Samuel 3, Lady 8/12 (85)
FONVILLE, W. G. 36 (m), M. A. 30 (f), W. D. 7 (m), M. A. 10/12 (f) (42)
FORTNER, Jo 28*, Kisirer 30 (86)

FORTNER, W. W. 58 (m)*, Mary 45, Thomas 21, Mary 18, James 16, Martha 13, Ely 10 (93)
FORTNER, Wm. 25, Eliza 23, Lonzo 6, Wm. 1, infant 1/12 (f) (86)
FOULER, M. E.? 43 (f), A. J. 20 (f), I. M. 18 (m) (72)
FOWLER, C. D. 69 (m)*, D. C. 58 (f) (82)
FOWLER, J. T.? 32 (m)*, M. O.? 24 (f), D. A. 3 (f), N. A. 2 (f), S. A. 1 (f) (82)
FOWLER, M. H. 31 (m), P.C.S.?J. 27 (f), M. E. K. 9 (f), J. J. 7 (m), F. R. 5 (f), C. W. J. 4 (m), L. L. 1 (m) (82)
FOWLER, N. J. 39 (m), L. J. 36 (f), M. J. 15 (f), J. F. 12 (m), S. L. 9 (f), T. J. D. 7 (m), F. L. 4 (m) (82)
FRANKS, H. H. 35 (m), Adaline E. 44, F. M. 10 (m), David H. 7, Lucy L. 4 (90)
FRAZIER, John R. 35*, Melvina C. 39, William A. 12, Mary E. 10, Rily A. 6 (40)
FREEMAN, Jackson 68, Jane 56, Nancy E. 21, Perry M. 17 (5)
FREEMAN, Newton 18* (48)
FRIZZELL, Hugh 42, F. D. 40 (f), M. J. 18 (f), M. F. 15 (f) (45)
FRIZZELL, J. 52 (f), J. J. 20 (m), G. W. 18 (m), H. A. 27 (f) (84)
FRIZZELL, J. A. 30 (m), Margart 33, Wm. A. 6, John T. 2, U. G. 4/12 (m) (47)
FRY, Griffen 18?* (88)
FRY, James 23, Bittie 20, Ruba M. 1 (f) (90)
FRY?, J. H. 50 (m), Nancy 48, John W. 20, Bular 12, H. J. 10 (m) (88)
FRYAR, Henry C. 25, Elizabeth 27, Sarah 1, James M. 40 (57)
FRYAR, Rutha 60 (B), Cordelia 18, John 16, Martha 1 (48)
FRYER, Dilcy 65 (B), Bose 17, John 12 (39)
FUGG?, Mollie 19* (22)
FULLERTON, I. 44 (f), W. R. 17 (m), E. 11 (m), E. 11 (m) (67)
FULLERTON, J. R. 20 (m)* (67)
FUNDERBURK, Add 23 (m) (B), Mary C. 25, Albert A. 4, L. M. C. 3 (f), George W. 1, Ann 40 (43)
FUNDERBURK, Anny 20* (B), Mary 2 (55)
FUNDERBURK, David S.? 43, Louisa 39, Henritta 20, Esther A. 18, James S. 14, Amon 12, Louisa 6, Ella 2, David B. 75 (43)
FUNDERBURK, Sam 18* (B) (59)
FUSSLE, Martha J. 46, Marth C. 17, William J. 9, James C. 5 (1)
FUSSLE, Robert J. 22 (1)
FUSSLE, Samuel H. 20 (1)
GABBARD, W. T. 37 (m), M. J. 33? (f), E. 15 (f), J. W. 13 (m), M. 9 (f), T. 8 (m), J. E. 6 (m), D. 3 (f), J. 1 (m) (71)
GALLIOND?, E. R. 25 (f), S. V. 22 (f), M. A. 2 (f) (83)
GAMBLE, Sophrona 21*, Laura F. 19, Aaron B. 17, Ira 2/12 (23)
GARDNER, Martha A. 29* (33)
GARRARD, Mason 85* (B), Rachel 70, John 30, George 28, John 22, Robert 19 (28)
GARRATT, John 78, Jennie 70, Lenard 18 (46)
GARRATT, Samps 66 (B), Manda 35, Saml. 18, Rebecca J. 20, Cassa 14, Cora 10, Joana 9 (46)
GARRETT, M. A. 37 (f), M. L. 14 (f), M. E. 12 (f), N. E. 10 (f), A. Bennet 7 (f) (46)
GARRETT, R. H. 42 (m)*, Huldy 35, J. W. 12 (m), L. F. 10 (f), I. J. 8 (f), J. W. 5 (m) (63)
GATES, Lycurgus 33*, Emely 27, Lucinda 10, Sophia 7, Mary 5, Victora 3, Jacob 6/12 (41)
GAULT, Robt. 56*, Mary 40, Jlohn 22, Wm. 16, James 14, Richard 14?, Saml. 10, Alda 3,

Sarah 6, Olie 4 (f), George 2 (85)

GETTRING, Elmira D. 56, Fannie E. M. 46 (14)

GETTRING, Milton C. 48, Frances I. 29, George W. 7, Roeina 4, Amanda C. 2, Ocora 1/12 (14)

GIBBON, James 56, Mary A. 56, Nancy C. 16, James R. 14 (26)

GIBSON, Ater? 45 (m), Cintha A. 45, Henderson 18, Caroline 13, Mela 11, Mary 9, Charles 4 (89)

GIBSON, Henry 20, Lueza 18, Frances 11/12 (88)

GIBSON, James 26, Caroline 26, Sarah V. 3, Penny 7/12 (m) (89)

GIBSON, Steven 74*, Malisse 50 (92)

GILBERT, Gilbert 65 (B), Lotty 50 (1)

GILBERT, James F. 38*, Susan O. 39 (10)

GILL, Mary J. 16* (13)

GILLICK, George 17* (B) (20)

GIPSON, Bie 26 (m)* (60)

GIPSON, C. 42 (m), A. B. 41 (f), S. A. 17 (f), M. F. 16 (f), E. S. 14 (f), Leona 12, O. O. 9 (f), B. A. 6 (f), J. T. 4 (m), P. E. 2 (m) (65)

GIPSON, L. A. 18 (m), M. 18 (f) (68)

GIPSON, M. 43 (m)*, M. A. 36 (f), J. W. 13 (m), M. N. 11 (f), N. A. E. 9 (f), A. A. 5 (m), J. L. 3 (m) (69)

GIPSON, M. C. 24 (m)*, R. E. 47 (f), M. F. 2 (f) (63)

GIPSON, M. C. 66 (m)*, Sousner? 59 (f), W. T. 22 (m), M. A. 34 (f), Travis 12, J. T. M. 10 (m) (83)

GIPSON, N. 40 (f)*, J. L. 1/12 (m) (68)

GIPSON, N. 44 (f), P. 23 (f), H. 22 (f), M. 21 (f) (68)

GIPSON, Tobias 64, Jenny 47, J. B. 11 (f) (65)

GITTRING, Joseph J. 50, Hannah E. 28, George F. 19, Troy R. 14, Robert 10, Milton S. 9, Maneva A. 7, Martha J. 6 (14)

GOADING, R. 66 (f)*, P. 35 (m) (76)

GOFF, John R. 29, Mary E. 27, Caroline 7, Miner 1 (f) (52)

GOFF, Leander W. 25, Elizabeth 27, John W. 6, Mary E. 3, Lewis L. 13/30 (32)

GOFF, Lewis 66*, Marinda 57, Albert 19 (32)

GONDEL?, Manda J. 12* (12)

GOOCH, Geo? 18* (67)

GOOCH, W. C. 41 (m), Martha J. 42, John W. 20, George P. 18, Sidny J. 16, James E. 13, Willis C. 11, Thomas F. 9, Verona J. 1 (92)

GOODIN, Eph 22, Etta 21 (49)

GOODIN, G. J. 37 (m), Nancy 44, James 13 (49)

GOODMAN, John D. 30, Alvenda 26, Charles 6, William 3, Amon 1 (34)

GOSSET, Jake 30 (B), E. 24 (f), W. 10 (m), F. R. 3 (f), S. A. 2 (f) (69)

GOTHHARD, C. 9 (f)* (78)

GRAHAM, J. C. 17 (m)*, W. J. 14 (m) (60)

GRAHAM, W. H. 55 (m), M. J. 45 (f) (76)

GRAMMER?, Wm. 20, Bettie 23 (91)

GRAVES, E. 66 (f), M. A. 40 (f), M. C. 31 (f), J. M. 8 (m), B. G. 6 (m) (78)

GRAVES, Frona 26* (B) (59)

GRAVES, G. W. jr. 27 (m), M. C. 36 (f), L. C. 5 (m), W. C. 4 (m), A. E. 2 (f), Silvester 3/12 (79)

GRAVES, G. W. sr. 36 (m), M. T. 22 (f) (79)
GRAVES, R. L. 27 (m), M. E. 25 (f), L. C. 6 (f), A. M. 4 (f), J. C. 2 (m), F. E. 9/12 (f) (83)
GRAVES, S. C. 49 (f), J. L. 15 (m), A. J. 20 (m), J. J. 12 (m), B. F. 9 (m) (78)
GRAVES, T. 48 (f), G. W. 15 (m), Nan 13, M. A. 11 (f), I. M. 7 (f) (79)
GREEN, Powel W. 40, Virginia C. 40, George W. 12, Andrew N. 9, John H. 7, Frances I. 6, Susan A. 6 (30)
GREENWAY, E. 30 (f)* (91)
GREENWAY, E. C. 19 (f)* (64)
GREENWAY, J. 52 (m), Jane 37, G. W. 16 (m), M. A. 12 (f), M. E. S. 11 (f), N. N. 8 (f), J. M. 2 (m), S. R. 2/12 (m) (68)
GREENWAY, R. 25 (f)* (64)
GREENWAY, Wm. M. 27, M. J. 16 (f), Alis P. 3/12 (60)
GREEWAY, _____ 25 (f)* (90)
GRIFFIN, Mary 45* (21)
GRIFFIN, W. T.? 20 (m), R. M. 40 (f) (45)
GRIFFITH, Robert P. 51* (57)
GRIGGS, J. J. 41 (m), M. V.? 37 (f), W. R. 13 (m), L. E. 12 (f), D. B. 11 (f), J. E. 5 (m), Granvil 7, H. A. 6 (f), F. E. 2 (m) (61)
GRIGGS, Prissilla 42*, Elex 21, Wm. 19, Bray 10, Lorenzo D. 8, John 6 (89)
GRIGSBY, Lewis 21 (B), Dorcas 21, Minnie 4 (21)
GRIMES, James B. 21?, Minerva A. 19, James D. 1/12, Mary E. 58, David S. 21, George W. 19 (36)
GRINDSTAFF, Louisa 40*, Sarah F. 14, Lola M. 10, Benjamin 3 (32)
GRISSOM, Thos. 25 (B), Ange 24, Walter T. 2 (46)
GRONAMIN?, L. 40 (f)* (91)
GUILFORD, James E. 32*, Anner B. 24, Thomas D. 12, Franis M. 9, Wm. G. 1, Charles E. 5/12 (42)
GULLEGE, J. 59? (m), E. 46 (f), J. W. 20 (m), E. 18 (m), J. D. 12 (m), S. 10 (f), N. M. 7 (f), H. F. 4 (m) (72)
GULLEGE, J. L. 25 (m), M. A. 20 (f), C. 4 (m), S. E. 3 (f) (72)
GULLEGE, V. 44 (f), S. A. 22 (f), M. 20 (f), R. 17 (m), J. H. 16 (m), W. 14 (m), M. 10 (f), J. 7 (m) (72)
GULLEGE, Wm. 30, J. A. 26 (f), L. A. 9 (f), M. L. 7 (f), M. A. 5 (f), W. T. 3 (m), S. L. 1 (m) (72)
GURLEY, Benjn. 13* (54)
GURLEY, Isham G. 35*, Nancy C. 34, Jorallis 12, Frances J. 11, Robert W. 8, Sylvester 6, William 1 (2)
GURLEY, James 62, Sarah 50, Willis 17, Benjamin 12, Henry 9, Jackson 7 (34)
GUTHRIE, Anna 32* (B), Mary M. 6, Ulysis S. 5 (26)
HAGGARD, C. H. 30 (m), Lucinda 28, M. C. 6 (f), M. A. 5 (f), S. J. 3 (f), V. E. 1 (f) (48)
HAGGARD, G. W. 22 (m), B. A. 18 (f) (44)
HAGGARD, J. P. 43 (m), N. D. 41 (f), P. 4 (m), S. 12 (m) (72)
HAGGARD, John S. 20, Martha E. 23, Eliza A. 1, Mary E. 4/12 (38)
HAGGARD, M. E. 40 (f)* (48)
HAGGARD, Rebecca 60, Elizabeth 24 (47)
HAINS, J. A. 33 (m), M. A. 31 (f), M. N. 11 (f), M. W. 9 (m), J. E. 7 (m), S. W. 4 (m), Deodatus? 2 (m) (64)
HALBROOK, Henry 50, Rebecca 44, Sarah J. 23, William 19, Elisabeth 17, George 15,

Franklin 13, Emely 6, Rebecca 3, Martha 10/12, John 21 (39)
HALEY, Emily K. 73* (55)
HALEY, Manuel 40 (B), Martha 43, Philip 16, George 12, Lucy 10, Jack 30 (55)
HALL, Elizabeth 66*, Edgar 13 (87)
HALL, Hannah 35 (B), Jane 16, Nichodemus 9/12, Mary M. 9/12 (39)
HAMER, Dr. 52*, Caroline 56, Ider 16 (87)
HAMLET, Austin W. 54, Amanda J. 37 (25)
HANCOCK, J. C. 33 (m)* (74)
HANCOCK, Joel C. 74* (30)
HANCOCK, Samuel S. 40*, Evaline C. 34, Nancy I. 8, Joel C. 4 (16)
HANES, Geo. W. 58*, Susan 52 (85)
HANES, Gloce? 65 (m), Christine 59, Lundar? 12 (f), P. 29 (m), Hiram L. 24, John 22 (91)
HANES, Griffin 33, Martha A. 28, Florence 8, Ider 5, Samuel 1/12 (92)
HANES, Tom? 28, Sarah C. 26, Wm. H. 4, Claudie 2, Mary J. 5/12 (91)
HANEY, Ellen 40*, Margaret 8, Mary J. 6, Lucy 4 (13)
HANEY, Wesley 15* (53)
HANEY?, Sarah 77* (13)
HANNAN, B. 20 (m) (B), R. A. 18 (f) (80)
HARAWAY, Aza H. 13* (6)
HARAWAY, Mary A. 45, James S. 16, Nancy E. 10 (15)
HARDCASTLE, John 44, Charity 28, Eliza C. 24, Mary E. 3/12 (34)
HARDEN, Alexander 56, Martha J. 38, Smith H. 20, Charles T. 14 (34)
HARDEN, Jane 30* (12)
HARDER, J. F. 28 (m)*, Paralle 21, Robt. L. 3, Huldah E. 1 (19)
HARDEY?, G. W. 61 (m), Nancy 58, George 19, Charles 18 (89)
HARDIN, A. 51 (m), H. C. 26 (f), Newton 17, Suannah 15, Leondas 11, Mary E. 7, Lucyh 5, F. C. 3 (f) (86)
HARDIN, J. L. 19 (m)* (48)
HARDIN, Sarah J. 36, William L. 16, Joseph 14, Eugene 12, Cornelis 6 (37)
HARDIN, T. G. 34 (m)*, Margarett D. 38, William T. 10, Leona 8, Vannie A. 4 (20)
HARDIN, T. Wade 45, Luraney 43, Martha A. 15, Jas. M. 13, Sarah J. 10, Charles F. 8 (52)
HARE, Henry H. 35* (34)
HARINGTON, James 32*, Martha 36, S. E. 12 (f), A. E. 9 (f), N. I. 6 (f), J. H. 5 (m) (78)
HARINGTON, W. 30 (m)*, D. A. 34 (f), E. 60 (f) (78)
HARIS, Ann 30 (B), M. J. 4 (f) (69)
HARIS, E. H. 27 (m)*, M. J. 28 (f), M. F. 8 (f), J. W. 6 (m) (64)
HARIS, J. H. 21 (m)*, J. J. 18 (m), W. E. 11 (m), A. J. 5 (m) (63)
HARIS, W. B. 44 (m), M. E. 38 (f), Basetta? 14, C. W. 18 (m), Bellsa? 11 (f), Mary 9, Alice 7, James 6, Albert 3, Leanna 1 (65)
HARMON, Bill 25* (B) (59)
HARMON, C. M. 62 (m)*, S. A. 29 (f), Eliza 32, Brunett 4 (f), Sallie 2, Sam 10 (B) (45)
HARPESS?, Andrew 36, Ive 20 (f), Taury B. 10 (f), Eliza 8, James 6, Ader 1 (34)
HARREL, William T. 22*, L. Frances 32, Robert E. 11/12 (3)
HARRELL, Geo. S. 35, Margrett 33, John W. 11, Thos. S. 9, Margrett L. 7, Mary E. 5, Wesley 2, Jas. E. 8/12 (52)
HARRELL, George W. 67*, Margret 63 (53)
HARRELL, M. 34 (f) (B), W. 13 (m), E. 4 (m), M. A. 3 (f), A. F. 1 (f), T. 22 (m), G. 20 (m) (70)

HARRELL, N. C. 33 (m), Nancy C. 34, Mary J. 8, Amanda A. 7, Maggie B. 3 (52)
HARRINGTON, F. Marion 28, T. Lillian 27, J. Marion 8, Magnolia 6, Jas. F. 4, N. M. E. 3 (50)
HARRINGTON, James 18, Elizabeth 18 (49)
HARRINGTON, Nancy 51*, Vicy A. 24, Fayette V. 19 (47)
HARRINGTON, S. J. 34 (m), A. E. 23 (f), M. A. 9 (f), A. L. 6 (f), W. J. 3?, C. J. 3/12 (f) (50)
HARRINGTON, Wm. jr. 24, Mary 22, Wm. 3?, A. J. 1 (f) (48)
HARRINGTON, Wm. sr. 60, J. F. 20 (m), Marshall 15, Cordelia 12 (49)
HARRIS, Berry 30* (92)
HARRIS, S. G. 62 (m)*, C. L. 45 (f) (82)
HARRIS?, M. P. 30 (m)*, M. A. 22 (f), Dora 5, Lena 2 (93)
HARROWAY, Anna 21* (51)
HART, Briant F. 24, Sary E. 26, Mary A. 2 (1)
HARTLEY, E. F. 31 (m)*, Lucy 27, Cora 6, Rora 4 (m) (93)
HARTLEY, Thos. J. 35, Nannie 26, Willie 12, Lillie 7, Smilie? A. 5 (m), Adar 3, Ider 1 (86)
HARTT?, J. A. 42 (m), Lucinda 35, John F. 13?, Wm. H. 12, Sidney 10, Aaron C. 6, Callie D. 3, Monro P. 7/12 (93)
HARWELL, William A. 36, Nancy A. 34, William P. 13, James S. 11, Thomas A. 8, Joseph S. 1 (5)
HAWKS, John 26*, M. J. 20 (f), R. W. 4 (m), E. E. 11/12 (f) (72)
HAWKS, T. 22? (m), A. 22 (f), E. M. __ (m) (71)
HAWKS, W. H. 50 (m)*, E. C. 45 (f), J. 16 (m), F. W. 11 (m), E. A. 9 (m) (72)
HAY, Henery J. 26, Maranda 25, Thomas 8, John 6, Benjamin 4, Adar 1 (17)
HAY, Mary H. 17* (13)
HAY, Thomas 78, Mary D. 51, George W. 31, Emily 30, Cordelia 20 (17)
HAY, William 44*, Martha 41, Martha C. 16, Samuel R. 14 (58)
HAYES, A. 19 (m)* (70)
HAYES, H. Em 37 (m), S. 36 (f), T. R. 17 (m), I. 14 (m), D. 12 (m), T. 11 (f), C. 9 (f), J. 2 (m) (71)
HAYS, A. 18 (m)* (82)
HAYS, A. 45 (m), E. A. 54 (f), M. G. 33 (m), J. M. 18 (m), M. C. 16 (f), E. O. 6 (m) (84)
HAYS, A. M. 24 (m)*, M. M. 33 (f), J. N. 6 (m), L. W. 4 (m) (84)
HAYS, A. M. 41 (m), M. A. 32 (f), M. P. 9 (f), J. P. T. 1 (m), A. P. H. 2/12 (m) (81)
HAYS, B. T. 48 (m), Mary 48, M. I. 18 (f), J. T. 16 (m), A. V. 13 (f), M. W. 11 (f), B. J. 10 (m), E. G. 5 (m), G. H. 2 (m), M. 66 (f) (83)
HAYS, E. 63 (m)*, M. A. A. 43 (f), B. M. 16 (f), M. J. 14 (f), W. E. 12 (f), S. W. 10 (f), P. A. 8 (f) (83)
HAYS, E. B. 10 (f)* (81)
HAYS, Granvil 24* (49)
HAYS, I. M. 40 (m), M. E. 41 (f), J. B. 22 (m), S. N. jr. 20 (m), S. L. 18 (m), Josep 16 (f), M. E. 14 (f), T. J. 13 (m), A. E. 11 (f), R. A. 8 (f), A. P. 5 (f), M. F. 1 (f), J. D. 3/12 (m) (81)
HAYS, J. A. 21 (m)*, M. J. 33 (f), M. R. B. 8 (f), C. L. 4 (m), V. J. 10/12 (f) (80)
HAYS, J. B. 23 (m)* (82)
HAYS, Juda 12 (f)*, Robert 10, Martha 6, Sarah 4, E. J. 6/12 (f) (78)
HAYS, M. B. 27 (m), Ana 22, Charlottee 5, M. J. 3 (f), W. G. 1 (m) (81)
HAYS, T. 12 (f)* (82)
HAYS, W. A. 25 (m), Levena 30, M. R. 18 (f), E. N. 11 (m), M. A. 10 (f), S. L. 9 (m), O. K.?

5 (m) (80)
HEARN, W. D. 25 (m)* (43)
HELM, William H. 52, Nancy L. 50, Fannie? J. 15, George W. 12, Lydia A. 8 (2)
HELMER, Rebeca R. 45 (17)
HELMS, Luther M. 25, Eliza A. 21, Rosaella 5, Riley M. 11/12 (7)
HENDRIX, H. A. C. 50 (m)*, J. D. 20 (f), J. B. 9 (f), M. 5 (f) (64)
HENDRIX, Ham? 19* (64)
HENDRIX, J. C. 30 (m), T. 36 (f), L. 12 (f), R. 11 (f), E. 10 (f), J. 8 (f), M. 5 (f), S. 3 (m), Thos. 2 (69)
HENDRIX, J. N. 35 (m), M. J. 24 (f), Ida 6, L. E. 5 (f), W. P. 4 (m), D. D. 2/12 (m), E. 55 (f), L. G. 12 (m) (63)
HENDRIX, M. M. 50 (f), M. C. 29 (f), Martha C. 27, L. J. 22 (f), Jas. M. 19, S. J. 16 (f), Emma 13, Alice 9 (48)
HENDRIX, N. 8 (f)* (64)
HENDRIX, S. W. 53 (f), S. J. 17 (f) (60)
HENDRIX, W. P. 28 (m), L. T. 28 (f), Wm. G. 7, J. M. 5 (m), Louella 2 (64)
HENDRIX, Wiley 27* (47)
HENNING, Malinda 46, Andrew J. 16, Wiley W. 13 (6)
HENSLEY, Joel H. 26, Nancy 18, Sary E. 5 (6)
HENSLEY, M. G. 25 (m)* (93)
HENSLEY, Sarah E. 18?, Ben 16, Wm. 13, Dona 11 (47)
HENSON, John 34*, Jane 42 (23)
HERNDON, C. C. sr. 61 (m)*, Jane 45, E. E. 27 (f), C. C. jr. 22 (m), G. J. 19 (f), A. A. 17 (f), W.? G. 14 (m), M. E. 6 (f), J. W. 1 (m) (79)
HERNDON, L. B. 24 (m), E. E. 22 (f) (79)
HICKERSON, W. B. 22 (m), Amanda 19, Sallie C. 8/12 (22)
HILL, Charles 52* (B), Tempa 39, Augusta 10, Izabell 8, Leonard 6, Ater 5 (f), Pink 3 (m), Maggie 1 (30)
HILL, D. 64 (m)*, M. 63 (f) (68)
HILL, Georgian A. 28*, Mary 7, Thomas W. 5 (17)
HILL, J. T. 40 (m), Josepheen 40, G. H. 18 (m), L. V. 16 (f), H. B. 14 (m), C. H. 12 (f), W. M. 10 (m), M. P. 4 (f) (83)
HILL, J. W. 25 (m)*, I. 19 (f), E. 2 (m), R. 5/12 (f) (68)
HILL, John 33*, Mary A. 28, Oscar 5 (92)
HILL, Joseph A. 33*, Minnie L. 5, Mary A. 2 (21)
HILL, Maggie 6* (10)
HINEMAN?, John B. 59* (88)
HOBBS, T. H. 32 (m), F. J. 28 (f), W. H. 12 (m), J. R. 10 (m), A. B. 4 (f), Ider May 3/12 (48)
HOLDER, Abram 30* (B), Amanda 25, William 5, John 3, Mary E. 2, Henry W. 2/12 (19)
HOLIWAY, W. 27 (m), B. E. 28 (f), A. M. 9 (f), W. E. 8/12 (m) (67)
HOLLAND, Asah 41, Mary 42, Elizabeth 14, Molly E. 10, Witt 6, Cora 2 (9)
HOLLAND, Ephraim M. 32, Frances E. 40, Benjamin F. 20, Samantha C. 8, James O. 7, Luana V. 4, Mary E. 2 (4)
HOLLAND, James M. 46, Eliza J. 41, Jessee T. 14, Richard A. 6 (31)
HOLLAND, John D. 37, Catherine 35, Bettie 10, John L. F. 7, Elvira 60 (6)
HOLLAND, John M. 36, Frances A. 30, Perry I. 7, Johny M. 5, Evrett A. 3, Walter C. 3/12 (33)
HOLLAND, Levi 22, Winny P. 18, Sylvester 1 (5)

HOLLAND, Maston 72, Nancy 47 (9)
HOLLAND, William 23, Fannie 24 (32)
HOLLAND, William 66*, Martha 60, Alfred 32, James S. 30, Anderson L. 26, Wiley B. 22, Malissa A. 19 (32)
HOLLAND, William F. 34*, Mary E. 36, Emily E. 10, James E. 8, William S. 5 (32)
HOLLEY, Geo. C. 25, Nancy 21 (48)
HOLLEY, J. W. 59 (m)*, N. Jane 47, Jessee A. 15, Elizabeth 11, Dona Bell 7 (48)
HOLLY, J. M. 36 (m), M. E. 31 (f), Wm. Lewis 6, Jas. L. 4, Wesley F. 2 (45)
HOLMES, Jessee 46, Cintha E. 40, Pleasant W. 15, Edward W. 8, Ida 3 (7)
HOLT, George 30 (B), Hannah 28, Henry 3, Edward 1, Elizabeth R. 1/12 (28)
HOMER, Thomas 32 (B), Jane 40, Thomas 14, William 12 (40)
HOOSER, Thomas J. 57, Hannah E. 35, John W. J. 14, Thomas 9, Martha J. 7, Hester T. 2/12 (9)
HOPKINS, George 30*, Anna A. 27, Eliza V. 7, William W. 1 (21)
HOPPER, J. Thomas 27, Matilda J. 24, Wm. Thos. 9, Marietta 5, James F. 2, John H. 9/12 (53)
HOPPER, J. W. 50 (m), Mary A. 52, Martha C. 22, John 14, J. W. 13 (m), Ira M. 10, Wiley M. 8 (53)
HOPPER, Samuel H. 18, Southa? M. 18 (f), Sophronia 2/12 (55)
HOPPER, Sarah 57, Millard F. 23, Mitchell 9 (33)
HOPPER, William J. 22*, Christena 17, Martha E. 2 (59)
HOPPER, Winfield S. 33, Mary Jane 35, Ader 14, Robert 12, Mattie 10, Less 9 (f), Henry Lee 1, Joseph 1/12 (33)
HORTON, Marcus D. L. 34, Ellen H. A. 28, Dorah A. 8, John R. 7, William H. 3 (37)
HOUSTON, Dave 18* (B) (74)
HOUSTON, E. 24 (m)* (B) (76)
HOUSTON, J. 25 (m)* (B) (69)
HOUSTON, J. G. 56 (m)*, Martha 56, J. C. 24 (m), E. J. 20 (m), W. F. 13 (m) (74)
HOUSTON, J. N. 65 (m), S. E. 35 (f), J. F. 14 (m), T. E. 13 (m), L. B. 12 (f), C. H. 10 (m), J. C. 8 (m), C. L. 5 (f), A. L. 5 (m), C. K. 3 (m), M. M. 1 (f) (60)
HOUSTON, J. P. 58 (m), Jane 60, M. J. 22 (f), W. M. 20 (m) (80)
HOUSTON, J. R. 32 (m), M. E. 32 (f), M. L. 9 (m), M. A. 7 (f), A. J. 5 (f), S. A. 3 (f), H. E. 8/12 (f) (79)
HOUSTON, Jefferson P.? 24* (57)
HOUSTON, John L. 28, Martha J. 22, Marcus D. L. 5, Elnora 3, Ella 1 (38)
HOUSTON, Pier 66? (m) (B), Parthenia 56, Roena 16 (42)
HOUSTON, S. L. 29 (m), L. C. 22 (f), T. W. 7 (m), V. E. 4 (f), E. M. 1 (f) (75)
HOUSTON, S. M. 41 (m)*, M. H. 41 (f), H. J. 16 (m), J. F. 14 (m), E. J. 12 (m), E. J. 10 (f), M. R. 8 (f), W. E. 4 (m), N. S. 3 (m), Ara 8/12 (f) (77)
HOWARD, M. 61 (f)* (83)
HOWELL, Christopher C. 32, Margaret E. 21, James G. 1, Sarah E. 4/12 (9)
HOWELL, Elijah G. 24 (9)
HOWELL, J. E. 31 (m), P. E. 29 (f), A. E. 11 (f), W. H. 8 (m), J. M. 5 (f), L. P. 1 (f) (65)
HUCKABA, Allen 18* (29)
HUCKABA, Charnall 45, John A. 21, Henry Clay 17, Virginia A. 16, Sarah F. 14 (30)
HUCKABA, James M. 18* (30)
HUCKABA, John W. 51, Sarah A. 31, William 14, Henrietta 10, Thomas W. 8 (30)
HUGHES, Cesar 40* (B), Lavina 30, Frances 12, Estilee 10, Nancy 4 (21)

HULME, H. L. 30 (m) (86)
HULME, L.? M. 26 (m) (86)
HULME, M. M. 33 (m)*, Jane 26, Cora 8, Dina 6, Linnie 11/12 (93)
HULME, R. C. 55 (m), Martha 54, Mattie 14, Thomas 7 (86)
HULME, T. D. 21 (m) (86)
HUNT, A. 49 (m), C. 18 (f), A. 3 (f) (73)
HUNT, Fannie 29*, Benona 7 (57)
HUNT, Louisa J. 40* (26)
HURN?, Thomas Y. 23, Nancy 22 (39)
HURST, G. 39 (m)* (74)
HURST, Nanny 27, Emer 11, Etter 7 (36)
HURST, Samuel K. 18* (7)
HUTSON, P. E. 51 (m), M. M. 48 (f), M. A. 16 (f), Robert 12, C. A. J. 8 (m) (44)
HUTSON, William 24, Mary E. 23, Bella M. 1 (58)
HYNES, Thomas 20* (6)
IVEY, B. F. 28 (m), A. A. 23 (f), R. W. 6 (m), Elmer 4 (70)
IVEY, James H. 35, Hariet M. 26, Safrona J. 14, Martha E. 10, John W. 6, James D. 4, George M. 1 (12)
IVEY, Jim 27* (51)
IVEY, John J. 53, Mary E. 43, Arra 14, Allice 13, William 7, Dolly 5, John W. 3, Emily 1 (12)
IVEY, Tennessee 35* (6)
IVEY, William R. 30, Milly M. 25, Martha J. 1 (12)
IVY, E. W. 15 (m)*, J. G.? 10 (m) (81)
IVY, F. M. 28 (m), Elisabeth 26, J. W. 2 (m) (78)
IVY, J. C. 40 (m)*, Martha 44, M. M. 14 (f), G. T. 12 (m), M. E. 10 (f), S. J. 8 (f), Paralee 6, W. B. 4 (m), N. S. 2 (m) (81)
IVY, M. 66 (m)*, L. L. 68 (f). R. M. 25 (m) (78)
IVY, M. 71 (f)* (83)
JACKSON, George A. 34*, Solin E. 13, Joacum D. 11 (19)
JACKSON, Jane 59, Mary 49. Mray E. 35 (17)
JACKSON, John H. 62, John A. 25 (17)
JACKSON, S. 72 (f), S. V. 21 (f), P. A. 18 (f), S. A. 17 (f), B. A. 10 (f), Parley 14 (f) (64)
JACKSON, Sary 66* (13)
JAGERS, James 14* (27)
JAMES, John R. 41, Annah 46, Nancy 13, John T. 10 (13)
JAMES, William 43*, Emily F. 16 (17)
JEANES, H. W. 10 (m)* (81)
JENNING, W. C. 57 (m), martha 45, William F. 19, Joseph Thomas 16, Marshal R. 11, Kiziah I. 8 (22)
JENNINGS, Ann 22 (B), Adline 9, S. J. 6 (f), Pinkney 8, D. F. 1 (f) (62)
JENNINGS, E. M. 65 (f)*, W P. 23 (m), R. A. 24 (f) (60)
JENNINGS, J. 35 (m) (B), M. J. 34 (f), J. T. 10 (m), A. J. 9 (m), D. F. 8 (m), Ida A. 6, S. W. 4 (m), M. E. 2 (f) (61)
JENNINGS, J. A. 14 (m)* (B) (83)
JENNINGS, J. E. 9 (m)* (B), Thos. E. 6, Fredonia 13, Mary 3 (61)
JENNINGS, J. H. 39 (m), M. E. 39 (f), S. A. 12 (f), M. E. 10 (f), E. C. 8 (f), J. H. 7 (m), W. W. 5 (m), L. L. 4 (m), C. C. 2 (f), Wells D. 21 (82)

JENNINGS, J. P. 30 (m) (B), N. 26 (f), J. 13 (m), S. E. 12 (f), Ann? 10, M.? F. 8 (m), C. 6 (m), H. 2 (m), S. 1 (m) (71)
JENNINGS, J. W. 48 (m), S. H. 40 (f), M. G. 20 (f), S. A. 18 (f), T.? S. 13 (m), E. E. 7 (f), H. A. 5 (m), F. B. 1 (f) (60)
JENNINGS, Louis 95 (B), M. A. 25 (f), R. L. 10 (m), R. J. 5 (f), M. M. 3 (f) (62)
JENNINGS, M. 18 (f)* (77)
JENNINGS, M. 24 (f) (B), M. J. 11 (f), Calvin 4 (62)
JENNINGS, S. T. 20 (m) (B), Mandy 17, W. I. 1 (m) (62)
JOBE, Susan 16* (B), James 9, Elizabeth 5/12 (21)
JOHNSON, A. L. 42 (m)*, Julia M. 44, M. J. 15 (f), Cordelia 10, Joseph L.? 9, Melvina 6, Eller J. 5, Milton A. 1 (45)
JOHNSON, A. N. 36 (m) (B), Charity 44, A. J. 15 (m), W. S. 14 (m) (83)
JOHNSON, Albert 16* (B) (59)
JOHNSON, Arta 8* (24)
JOHNSON, Arter 18 (m)* (B) (28)
JOHNSON, C. 18 (m) (B), M. A. 18 (f), R. B. 4/12 (f), M. 60 (f), M. J. 14 (f), F. 10 (f) (83)
JOHNSON, Ester 50 (B), John 22, Jose 18 (f), Lynn 10 (m), Nickolas 8, Oliver 6, Clauda 5 (m), Adam 3, Mattie 1 (25)
JOHNSON, Frances 45, William 20, Emerson E. 18, Christopher H. 16 (11)
JOHNSON, Geo. 50 (B), Narsis 30, C. R. 2 (f), G. W. 1 (60)
JOHNSON, H. 46 (m), F. F. 24 (f), M. C. 4 (f) (83)
JOHNSON, Hickman M. 22, Martha A. 18, Henery L. 7/12 (3)
JOHNSON, J. I. 28 (m), S. M. 29 (f) (67)
JOHNSON, J. M. 53 (m)*, N. A. 50 (f), W. G. 17 (m), N. E. 12 (f), E. E. 9 (f), F. 6 (f), J. T. 3 (m) (67)
JOHNSON, James 27, Catharine 27, Elizabeth A. 7, William J. 3, Charles 1 (26)
JOHNSON, Jessee 35, Mary B. 33, William A. 11, Mary F. 10, Richard 8, Eliza A. 6, John W. 1, James L. 3/12 (59)
JOHNSON, John 60, Sophia 54, Anguline 19 (23)
JOHNSON, John T.? 27, Lucy C. 24, Rufus V. 5, Joseph H. 2 (3)
JOHNSON, Jonas 17* (B) (30)
JOHNSON, Mahalia 16* (B) (28)
JOHNSON, Nora 17* (B) (28)
JOHNSON, Rufus J. 54, Elizabeth H. 52, Rufus B. 19, Nancy J. 17, Kiziar E. 14, Joseph L. 11, James M. 7, Jesse Z. 4, William H. 30 (3)
JOHNSON, S. 24 (m)* (B) (81)
JOHNSON, S. 66 (m)* (B), M. 50 (f), Henery 21 (83)
JOHNSON, Samuel 28, Elizabeth 32, John 9, Mollie 7, Tennie 4, Jinnie 1 (22)
JOHNSON, Sarah 17* (B) (30)
JOHNSON, T. 44 (m), C. 49 (f), J. N. 20 (m), M. A. E. 16 (f), J. W. 12 (m) (68)
JOHNSON, W. T.? 23 (m), I. 18 (f) (67)
JOHNSON, William 62, Nancy 38, Calvin 19, Tennessee C. 15, Walter H. 5, Alfred L. 3 (15)
JOHNSON?, Washington? 11*, Alison 8 (m), Noel 4 (53)
JONES, Archba. 61 (1)
JONES, Burell 45, Nancy 47, Allen 18, John 16 (16)
JONES, Calvin 42, Elisabeth 40, Lucy A. 18, Parlee 15, Una 9 (34)
JONES, Elenora 55*, Sarah E. 23, Churchwell G. 19, Rachael S. 15 (38)
JONES, Elias P.? 58 (3)

JONES, G. W. 24 (m)*, Lillian 18 (56)
JONES, Henry M. 33, Mary A. 32, Cora A. 7, Maggie P. 3, James H. 1 (54)
JONES, Ida 10* (B) (60)
JONES, J. Calvin 55, S. M. 43 (f), E. J. 24 (f), L. B. 20 (f), Josey 16, Matty 14, Emma E. 12, E. D. 3 (m) (47)
JONES, James L. 30, Margaret P. 24, Nora S. 4, Jammie M. 7/12 (11)
JONES, James W. 21* (43)
JONES, John A. 22, Mary K. 18 (59)
JONES, John H. 25 (1)
JONES, Mahalia 22* (46)
JONES, Martha 46* (59)
JONES, Martha A. 22*, Bede 19 (39)
JONES, Martin 32, Eliza 48 (39)
JONES, Mary 29, Josep 12, John 9, Martha 7, Franklin 2 (37)
JONES, N. E. 35 (f) (B), W. A. 18 (f), F. L. F. 14 (f), H. M. 8 (m), L. E. 5 (f) (62)
JONES, Rasbery F. 29, Edora T. 29, Arba? A. 2 (1)
JONES, Troy W. 44*, Flora 14 (57)
JONES, Vernid E. 28, Malisa A. 24, Josiah G. 6, Alice E. 2, Charles P.? 1 (3)
JONES, Will 19* (B) (62)
JONES, William R. 12* (17)
JONES, William T. 23, Nancy J. 24 (34)
JORDAIN, H. M. 36 (m)*, M. A. 35 (f), Lucy B. 14, Ephram 12, William 10, Alice 8, Aura 6, John 5, Albert 3, Charley 2, unnamed 5/12 (m) (61)
KEEN, Lucy 78, Elisabeth 47 (81)
KEEN, W. R. 34 (m)*, M. E. 27 (f), W. J. 10 (m) (81)
KEENE, Ferba 40* (51)
KEENE, Jerry 72, Mary 44, Asalim 14 (f), Marvel 5 (50)
KEETON, Albert F. 44, Parker D. 43, William R. 20, Lucy A. 19, Ellen U. 16 (29)
KEETON, John L. 54, Margaret M. 58, Sarah K. 17, William B. 16 (11)
KEETON, Robert F. 31 (11)
KEETON, Sanderson L. 20, Amanda E. 24, Margaret V. 8/12 (11)
KEETON, William 13*, Emily M. 12, John 7 (21)
KELLEY, Eber 48, Luhama 48, Felix H. 12 (10)
KELLEY, Elisha 39, Susannah C. 36, J. Lossen 15, Mary J. 13, Martha E. 11, Estelle O. 9, Reuben G. 7, Emily L. 5, Nanny F. 1 (8)
KELLEY, George 15* (15)
KELLEY, Jonas P. 21, Rebeca 21 (10)
KELLEY, Joseph 79, Dorcas A. 61 (4)
KELLEY, Judea 61 (8)
KELLEY, Mary E. 45, Sarah E. 14, Susannah 11, Florence 9, Riley D. 5 (10)
KELLEY, Riley G. 64*, Julia E. 49 (7)
KELLEY, Sarah 48, Genora 22, Ugene L. 20, Mary T. 16, Verta E. 13, Cora L. 10 (9)
KELLEY, William 30*, Caryezela 21, Frona V. 3 (6)
KELLEY, William D. 22, Nancy E. 25 (10)
KELLEY, William H. 25, Ellen 21 (8)
KELLY, Andrew J. 24, Mary A. 19, Andrew H. 7/12 (43)
KELLY, Angeline 49 (B), Samuel 22 (41)
KELLY, Christopher C. 33, Virginia 23, Cora A. 3 (37)

KELLY, Eliza 16* (B) (41)
KELLY, James 28, Nancy 27, Molly 7, John 5 (23)
KELLY, Kinchen 60*, Nancy M. 53, Norman L. 30, Mollie 27, Mary Jane 24, Daniel E. 21, Hetta S. 18 (31)
KELLY, Manuel 11* (B) (56)
KELLY, Mary 50*, Katharine 19, William J. 1 (23)
KELLY, Polli 54, Eliza 26, Louis C. 19, Elcie 5/12 (91)
KELLY, T. 30 (m) (B), M. G. 31 (f), F. G. 15 (f), M. C. 6 (f), Charles 2, Dave 3/12 (82)
KELLY, W. 35 (m), S. J. 30 (f), L. E. 9 (f), W. J. 3 (m), J. A. 1 (f) (76)
KELY, R. M. 30 (m)*, Martha A. 27 (91)
KEMP, John W. 60, Nancy C. 41, Wiliam 19, Laura I. 13, D? L. 10 (f), Udora G. 3 (15)
KEMP, William F. 18* (28)
KENDAL, Hugh L. 31, Sofrona 31, Martha A. 12, Hugh L. F. 10, Robert E. 7, Carter 2, Preston 2/12 (37)
KENDAL, John 50* (B), Sarah 45, Gurline 28, Green B. 17, John 13, Clark 9, Bethlehem 7, Bevel 5, Mary 1 (37)
KENDAL, Lucy A. 48, Margurete A. 25, Tabitha J. 21, Lewis F. 17, George W. 15, Madison 12, Matthew H. 12, Jonathan E. 8, Lucy S. 6 (37)
KENDAL, Martin J. 22, Harriett 21, Lewis J. 7/12 (41)
KENNEDY, Ahab? 22 (1)
KENNEDY, John F. 21*, Cora A. 18 (57)
KENNEDY, John G. 53, Mary J. 51, James W. 18, Ephraim C. 13, Thomas C. 11 (6)
KENNEDY, John J. 22 (6)
KENNEDY, Robert J. 79*, Cintha 71 (2)
KENNEDY, Shadr. H. 47, Martha A. L. 42, Samuel 20, Jesse M. 18, Shadrach M. 14, Cintha B. 11, Martha J. 10, George A. 7, Mary L. 5, James 2 (1)
KILPATRICK, William W. 37, Mary A. 40, George T. 12, James R. J. 11, Andrew J. 9, William D. 6/12 (26)
KIMBLE, George 13* (5)
KING, A. 59 (m)*, E. 58 (f), T. 15 (m) (B) (69)
KING, C. 31 (m)* (B) (72)
KING, G. W. 47 (m)* (78)
KING, Harriett 53* (B) (63)
KIRK, D. D. 22, Bettie 26, Maggie 4, Felix 2, Charles 1 (88)
KIRK, Frank 22, Mary J. 20, Joanne R. 1 (90)
KIRK, Wm. 52*, Sarah 49, Sallie 15 (88)
KIZER, Joe J. 60 (B), Jane 44, Joana 15, Laura 14, Lue 12 (f), Reuben 6, Thomas 3 (2)
KIZER, Vurnal 55, Lurrna E. 55, Nancy A. 15 (4)
KYLE, David 15* (22)
KYLE, Ursley 36, William T. 17, Ollie R. 1, Mary E.J.M.C. 13 (21)
LACKEY, James 54, Louvina J. 58 (5)
LACY, David W. 38, Margret P. 29, Harvey C. 12, Anne 11, Granvil H. 8, Mary A. 5, William H.? 3, Nancy B. 7/12 (54)
LACY, H. H. 25 (m), E. J. 21 (f), Lillian 1, N. F. G. 15 (m) (50)
LACY, Susan F. 43, W. Henry 27, J. Thomas 21, Nancy E. 19, John E. 16, N. F. G. 14 (m), Mary 12 (42)
LAFFERTY, Clinton 66*, Adaline C. 41, Racheal A. 12, Eliza J. 10, Cora L. 5, Oliver H. P. 2 (13)

LAIN, F.? D. 28 (m)*, Sallie 25, Mollie 8, Addie 5, Jula 8/12 (85)
LAIN, Thos. P.? 31, Fannie 32, Mollie 3, Louise 8/12? (85)
LAMROCK, John 58*, Sarah 47 (90)
LANCASTER, Benjamin M. 44, Martha T. 33, Robert L. 12, Emily C. 8, William E. 10/12 (11)
LANCASTER, David L. 73*, Cintha 61, Gabriel S. 22, Ervid 45 (9)
LANCASTER, Jesse J. 49, Susan E. 47, Tilman A. 21, Thomas E. 19, William 16, Jessee M. 13, John L. 10, Perry W. 7, David L. 3 (10)
LANCASTER, W. F. 45 (m), E. J. 28 (f), L. L. 8 (m), L. L. 5 (f), M. B. A. 1 (f) (80)
LARD, William F. 25, Josephine 21, Martha D. 4, Adar C. 3, Sherman C. 10/12 (6)
LASITER, Isabel 55* (43)
LASITER, John C. 36, Cintha E. 29, Mary F. 12, James R. 10, Emily E. 8, Mattie R. 5, Saffie E. 3, Ellie W. 1 (5)
LASITER, William 20*, Sarah F. 9 (38)
LASOM?, Abraham 40, Josephine 33, Harriett 13, Elmer 11, Lenora 10, Maude 8, Stewart 5, Lawrence 3, Dosey 1 (f) (53)
LASTER?, George 35, L. A. 29 (f), M. C. 13 (f), V.? R. 10 (f), J. A. 7 (m), S. W. 2 (m) (48)
LAWRENCE, T. D. 28 (m), E. J. 28 (f), Sammy 4, John A. 2 (60)
LAWS, Frances 66*, Mary E. 40, James 27, G. W. 25 (m), Leonard 23 (20)
LAWS, John 39*, Kittorah 27, Emily E. 8, Mary J. 5, Laura F. 3, George H. 1, John A. 4/12 (22)
LAWSON, N. 57 (f)*, Robert 16 (82)
LAY, Caroline E. 40* (26)
LEDFORD, T. J. 34 (m), N. P. 30 (f), A. A.? 12 (m), I. M. 10 (m) (81)
LEE, Ebenezer 57, Maney E. 39, Meilie? P. 14 (m) (7)
LEE, William B. 29*, Margarett J. 26 (7)
LENARD, B. M. 42 (f), M. R. 18 (f), P. E. 17 (f) (84)
LEWIS, Charlotte 35 (B) (17)
LEWIS, M. A. 63 (f), J. W. 18 (m) (64)
LEWIS, Thos. 30* (B) (75)
LEWIS, W. H. 42 (m), Harriet A. 38, Charles E. 13, Mary C. 11, Willie? P. 10, Thos. M. 8, Harvy G. 6, Robert L. 5, Laura M. 2 (90)
LILES, B. 64 (m), Serena 58, M. E. 34 (f), M. E. 29 (f), S. M. 26 (f), S. I. 19 (f), R. J. 13 (f) (78)
LILES, Minie 29* (43)
LILES, W. W. 38 (m), Mary F. 30, James A. 3 (43)
LINDSEY, Eli 25, Jane 22, Ovin L. E. 4, Molly A. 9/12 (37)
LISTON, M. A. 51 (f) (79)
LITTLE, Sarah 60, Martha 24 (56)
LIVINGSTON, J. G.? 33? (m)*, H. A. 33 (f), Ada 10, R. A. 10 (m), D. T. 7 (f), L. 3 (f), C. E. 3/12 (f) (62)
LIVINGSTON, J. P. 29 (m), S. E. 25 (f), W. S. 7 (m), L. J. 6 (m), C. A. 1 (f), E. 63 (f) (64)
LOCKHART, Benj. 21* (48)
LOFTEN, A. M. E. 55 (f), S. J. 28 (m), C. A. 14 (f), M. J. 11 (f) (80)
LOGAN, John B. 25* (31)
LOGUE, Henry 11* (51)
LOMAX, A. J. 26 (m), M. S. 24 (f), D. B. 6 (f), M. A. E. 3 (f), M. S. 4/12 (f) (79)
LOMAX, James 61?, A. E. 35 (f), M. J. 25 (f), W. H. 23 (m), M. M. 14 (f) (44)

LONG, G. F. 30 (m), R. M. 31 (f), L. B. 4 (f) (70)
LONG, G. F. 58 (m)*, L. A. 58 (f), M. 28 (f), M. A. 19 (f), H. W. 18 (m), W. S. 18 (m), M. J. 14 (f), E. V. 12 (f), G. D. 10 (m) (70)
LONG, G. W. 30 (m), M. A. 23 (f), W. F. 2, R. L. 2 (m) (70)
LONG, J. 22 (m)* (70)
LONG, J. W. 29 (m), M. M. J. 52 (f), M. A. 9 (f), F. E. 6 (f), A. J. 4 (m), A. L. 2 (f) (47)
LONG, Jno. A. 48, M. E. 24 (f), Wm. P. 15, J. H. 13 (m), Alonzo 5, Neeley 11/12 (f) (44)
LONG, S. G. 18 (m)* (63)
LOOPER, Sherod 51, Elizabeth 42, Gillum 20, George 18, Margret 16, Thomas 13, Elizar 12, Adar 11 (88)
LOOPER, Wm. 42*, Mary 37, Isabell 13, Emerson 10, P. A. 6 (f), Lavona 10/12 (88)
LORD, Catherine 25, Charles 5, S. A. J. 2 (f) (50)
LOVELL, Huston 50, Emeline 40, Bell 10, Sallie 7, Clementine 4, Patsie 76 (85)
LOVELL, _____ 65 (f)* (90)
LOWE, J. 17 (f)* (B) (82)
LOWE, M. T. 23 (f)* (60)
LOWE, P. L. 42 (f), George 13, Jessie 9, W. L. 4 (m), J. D. 3 (m) (81)
LOWERY, Hoad 39 (B), Matilda 43, Thomas J. 9 (2)
LOWERY, Jim 35 (B), Isibel 30, Houston 15 (2)
LOWERY, Sam 46 (B), Margaret 14, Pleasant T. 13, Hoad E. 12, John 9, Nancy 7, Robert 5 (3)
LOWERY, Sipio 67 (B), Eliza 25, Julia 22, Major 20, Charlotte 15, Isaac 8? (4)
LOWERY, Thomas 45, China 35, Sam 19, Martha 15, Tilda 14, Harrison 11, Josephine 10, Manda 9, Elizabeth 6, Robert M. 4, Elisha 2, Jasper 2/12 (2)
LUNN, H.? J. 30 (m), D. R. 20 (f), Cora L. 3 (87)
LUNSFORD, E. 44 (f), M. E. 7 (f), M. E. 6 (f), A.? W. 4 (m), J. P. 2 (m) (78)
LUNSFORD, E. 47 (f), G. W. 25 (m), N. J. 21 (f), B. J. 19 (f), H. E. 17 (f), J. R. 15 (m) (76)
LUNSFORD, J. C. 55 (m), L. S. 53 (f), E. C. 28 (f), E. C. 21 (f), A. G. 27 (m), M. C. 17 (m), A. J. 15 (m), D. A. 9 (m) (77)
LUNSFORD, J. S. 25 (m)*, M. J. 26 (f) (78)
LUNSFORD, J. W. 29 (m), M. D. 22 (f), W. W. 2 (m) (78)
LUNSFORD, W. P. 22 (m)*, K.? L. 21 (f), B. B. 1 (f) (78)
LUSTER, Jessee 38?* (B), Jane 30, Franklin 15, Andrew 13, George 11, John 10, Emily 8, Mary 6, William 4, Maggie 9/12 (55)
LUSTER, John 32*, Elizabeth 30, Margrett 9, Lora 7, Laura 5, Joseph 1 (59)
LUTON, Jonathan 56*, C. Cintha 40, M. E. 19 (f), Sallie M. 13, Amanda A. 11, Wm. O. 10, Auther M. 8, Stella A. 3?, Lillian G. 1 (54)
LUTON, Sampson 60* (B), Caroline 50, George 18, Emma 16, William 10 (54)
MADEN, L. R. 39 (m), Josie 26, D. 6 (m), Laura 3 (86)
MAHAN, Zilpha 67* (B) (30)
MAIDWELL, Alison W. 30, Sary E. 21, John W. 4, Albert T. 2, James G. 6/12 (5)
MAINESS?, M. K. 19 (f)*, M. C. 1 (f) (84)
MAJOR, Alexander 48* (B), Easter 45, John W. 17, James M. 15, Anna V. 13, Rufus H. 12, Lucy Jane 10, Granville 8, Nancy E. 6, Mary F. 4, Martha O. 1 (23)
MAJORS, Samuel H. 59, Jarah J. 22 (f), James W. 21, John T. 16, Adley O. 11 (m), Francis M. 7 (25)
MALONE, John 36, Amanda M. 27, William B. 24 (43)
MALONE, Nancy 56*, Lenora 20, Joseph 18, Cora E. 10 (43)

MALONE?, Louey 28*, Rebecca A. 30 (43)

MANES, James 37, Julia S. 29, Mary J. 12, William R. 8, John L. 7, Margaret 6, Sary E. 5, Benjamin F. 4, Dora E. 3, Earnest 1, Adar 1 (9)

MANESS, Angeline 13* (B) (56)

MANESS, Nathan S. 23 (6)

MANESS, Thomas J. 63, Elizabeth 54, Christiana 35, Elizabeth 28, Lucy A. 17, Charles 14, Gabriel 12, Thomas J. 8 (6)

MARCHBANKS, J. M. 19 (m)*, M. R. 16 (f) (62)

MARKUM, John 23, Julia 18, Josie 17, Arra 14, James 12 (93)

MARTIN, Frances A. 44, William H. 19, James H. 17, Nancy L. 16, Henery J. 11, Mary A. 8 (16)

MARTIN, George W. 25, Louisa T. 20, Arkansas S. 6/12, George G. 2 (7)

MARTIN, Isaac 27* (B), Lizzie 25, Fannie 3 (27)

MARTIN, Sary V. 47, Sary J. 23, James 14, Henery D. 18 (4)

MASSEY, James 26 (87)

MASSEY, Vinie 45, Margaret 28, Mary 22, Martha 19 (93)

MASSIE, R. 30 (m), M. S. 21 (f), E. 9/12 (f) (75)

MATHENA, John J. 22, Eliza A. B. 22, George W. 3 (11)

MATHES, Charles 18* (30)

MATHEWS, William 21, Nancy J. 22 (5)

MAUNEY, Abraham 53, Elizabeth M. 47, William M. 20, Abraham D. 18, Martha C. 15, John 13, Joseph M. 5, Maranda C. 2, Andrew F. 3/12 (1)

MAXFIELD, M. 45? (f), S. E. 18 (f), M. C. 16 (f), A. L. 13 (f), M. 11 (f), W. 11 (m), L. P. 9 (f), S. L. 7 (f), S. 5 (f) (70)

MAXWELL, T. 23 (m), W. F. 20 (f), E. J. 1 (m) (79)

MAXWELL, William S. 58* (58)

MAYO, Benjamin 45, Roda A. 18, Robert H. 12, William H. 9 (8)

MAYO, James W. 52, Mary E. 59, Bettie A. 20, Margaret C. 3, Emelilne 33 (8)

MAYO, William H. 30*, Nancy J. 29, James W. 3, Marietta 1 (8)

MAYS, A. 26 (m) (B), Meradis 20 (f) (77)

MAYS, H. 56 (f), J. W. 34 (m), B. A. 23 (m), C. P. 31 (m), M. A. 25 (f), M. C. 10 (f), Jessie 6, L. E. 4 (f) (77)

MAYS, P. 68 (m) (B), W. 20 (f), M. 15 (m), M. 4 (f), Jimie 2 (m) (77)

MAYS, Pleasant 20* (21)

MAYS, Rebecca 18* (26)

MAYS, S. 46 (m), S. M. 55 (f), H. S. 23 (f), M. E. 22 (f), M. J. 20 (f), Z.? H.? 14 (f) (74)

MAYS, W. G. 50 (m), R. L. 29 (f), A. W. 27 (m), M. J. 22 (f), A. G. 20 (m), W. A. 18 (m), M. J. 15 (m), M. B. 12 (f), L. M.? 9 (f) (76)

MAZE, E. 42 (m), J. A. 36 (f), W. 12 (m), M. L. 11 (f), S. B. 8 (m), E. E. 7 (m), M. J. E. 4 (f), S. S. 3 (m), J. F. 2 (m) (71)

MAZE, Thos. J. 33 (B), Marandy 35, J. A. 15 (m), E. C. 10 (f), L. T. 8 (m), G. H. 7 (m), M. E. 4 (f), J. P. 1 (m) (61)

MAZE, W. W. 36 (m) (B), Jane 36, J. W. 13 (m), N. A. 8 (m), T. C. 7 (f), E. F. 4 (f), Mary F. 1 (61)

MCANALLY, Elizabeth 61* (55)

MCBRIDE, Isaac R. 42, Nancy J. 37, William 11 (1)

MCBRIDE, Jane 40 (B), Louellen 14 (f), Jimmie 8, Henrietta 5, Michel H. 4, John E. 3/12 (29)

MCCALL, Daniel 23* (11)
MCCALL, Elisabeth J. 38, Hery C. 20 (m), Jef Davis 18, Moses C. 16, William R. 9, Mary 1, Tennessee 4 (B) (35)
MCCLANAHAN, Charles 42*, Martha 35, Henrietta 12, Cora 6, Minta 4, Dorah 1 (24)
MCCLANAHAN, Clumbus C. 41, Berthsheba 36, Gabriel F. 11, Mary J. 9, Berthsheba E. 6, Lorenah C. 2, Winny J. F. 5/12 (3)
MCCLANAHAN, David 35*, Margaret 30, Clara 9, John 8, James 17 (55)
MCCLANAHAN, Franklin L. 48, Caroline E. 46, Francis M. 22, Mary S. 19, Caroline E. 16, Martha J. 8 (6)
MCCLANAHAN, Granvel 32, Mary 23, Mattie 4, Murray 3, Allie 1 (10)
MCCLANAHAN, Joel H. 34, Rutha 28, Emma T. 5, Lilly F. 2, William J. 1 (23)
MCCLANAHAN, John 22*, Fannie 27 (24)
MCCLANAHAN, John W. 43, Ellen 39, John T. 7 (6)
MCCLANAHAN, Pinkney M. 38, Malinda J. 37, Benjamin F. 13, James A. 9, Mintee D. 8, Luellee 6, Leonard N. 2 (8)
MCCLARREN, Benj. F. 50 (15)
MCCLURE, C. A. 28 (m), Sarah 28, Flora L. 1, R. S. 11 (m) (46)
MCCLURE, D. J. 43 (m), Martha J. 35, Wm. Henry 14, Eunice A. 11, Doria J. 7, Nancy C. 5, Charles? 5/12 (52)
MCCLURE, Malinda 63* (12)
MCCLURE, W. C. 33 (m), N. S. 26 (f), E. L. 6 (f), A. A. 5 (f), J. B. 5 (f), S. D. 3/4 (f) (64)
MCCOLLOM, Alfied F. 59*, Emeline J. 55, Martha F. 15, Margaret M. 12 (7)
MCCOLLOM, Isaac F. 16* (7)
MCCOLLOM, James F. 25* (7)
MCCOMMACK, J. 24 (m)*, A. T. 21 (f), M. J. 7/12 (f) (60)
MCCORCLE, Allice 23* (B) (27)
MCCORCLE, Mose 53* (B), Ann 35, Lucy 12, William 10, Mary 8 (27)
MCCORKLE, Franklin B. 39, Mary 41, John F. 13, Sally A. 11, James E. 9, William R. 8, Thomas M. 5, George A. 9/12 (8)
MCCORKLE, McClain 29?* (54)
MCCORMAC, S. D. 36 (m), L. D. 26 (f), F. M. 6 (m), R. G. 5 (m), J. F. 8/12 (f) (79)
MCCORMACK, J. 23 (m), S. 23 (f), J. W. 2 (m), G. A. 3/12 (f) (66)
MCCULLEY, Allison B. 40*, Eliza C. 35, John W. 12, William L. 7, Mary E. 9, Virgel N. 1 (20)
MCDANIEL, Mollie 3* (90)
MCDANIEL, Newton 27* (31)
MCDANIEL, William 14* (22)
MCDONAL, P. 36 (m) (B), N. J. 30 (f), W. H. 12 (m), J. P. 8 (f), C. A. 5 (f), M. V. 3 (f) (80)
MCDONALD, Catharine 36* (27)
MCDONALD, F. 21 (m)* (B) (77)
MCDONALD, Mary E. 19* (13)
MCDONALD, William 52, James H. 27, John M. 16, Daniel 12, Luella 8 (16)
MCELRATH, Alf 33 (B), Elizabeth 28, Roenia 11, Albert 11, Mary E. 8, Minnie 7, Jessee 5, Richard 4, Roberta 1 (59)
MCELRATH, Baboy 22 (m)* (B) (57)
MCELRATH, Emeline 52 (B), Sophronia 17, Alice 16, Silva 25 (43)
MCELRATH, James 22 (B), Meriah 21, Eddy 1 (39)
MCELRATH, Peter 27 (B), Jane 21, Eveline 6, Mat A. 4, James 2, Cora M. 5/12 (37)

MCELWAIN, James 30, Susan 28, James M. 10, Minnie B. 8 (91)
MCGARVEY, Wasson? 54*, Margret 44, Jas. W. 10, M. E. 7 (f) (47)
MCGILL, Julia 19* (87)
MCKINY, Thomas E. 22* (26)
MCKNIGHT, Elijah 20* (46)
MCLAMORE, Peter 60 (B), Eveline 59, Pompy 21, Joseph 19 (38)
MCLEMORE, A. 27 (m)* (B), E. 19 (f), B. 2 (m), R. H. 6/12 (m) (78)
MCLEMORE, H. 26 (m)* (B), H.? J. 26 (f), A. 2 (f), C. 8/12 (f) (76)
MCLIMOR, M. L. 16 (f)* (78)
MCLIN, James 19, Babe 19, John 11/12, Jo 11/12 (m) (85)
MCMAKIN, Jasper 46, Mary E. 44, Mary J. 18, Frances 12, Letha E. 8, Rufus 6, Robert L. 3, Charley 1 (35)
MCMICKLE, J. B. 64 (m)*, R. A. 40 (f), C. 15 (f), A. 11 (f), S. B. 9 (m), A. 3 (m), E. 5/12 (m) (70)
MCMILLAN, John 57*, Mary A. 47, John G. 20, Wm. J. 18, Mary E. 12 (42)
MCMILLAN, Wm. H. H. 42, Rebecca 36, Martha E. 16, Emma M. 14, Mary K. 12, Charley A. 7 (f) (58)
MCMILLION, J. 49 (m), Ellen 40, T. B. 12 (m) (69)
MCMILLON, A. 82 (m)* (82)
MCMIN?, Elizabeth 22* (11)
MCMURRY, E. 50 (f)* (82)
MCMURRY, J. R. 26 (m)* (77)
MCMURRY, T. W. 48 (m), S. 45 (f), M. 15 (f), Gillie 14, Jennety 11, T. 8 (m), Dora 6, Mary 5, Claud 2 (69)
MCNIGHT, C. 21 (f)* (75)
MCPEAK, Jas. 24, S. E. 19 (f), John H. 3 (45)
MCWHIRTER, James W. 48, Nancy P. 39, James 17, Walter S. 14, Perry 12, Sarah E. 6, Jessee 3, Mary J. 1 (42)
MEDLIN, Viana J. 22, George C. 1 (1)
MEEK, Thomas 20* (B) (33)
MELTON, Abner 30*, Mary E. 26 (22)
MELYS?, J. 55 (m), J. I. 30 (m), W. C. 20 (f), E. P. 14 (m), W. J. 7 (m), G. 5 (m), S. E. 2 (f), M. A. 26 (f) (77)
MENS?, Antny 22* (B) (63)
MERRICK, Dock 37, Jinnie 32, Eular 8, Clora 6, Oscar V. 4, Roddy 2, Dazie 4/12 (87)
MERRYMAN, Catharine 30*, William F. 5 (23)
MERRYMAN, J. H. 22 (m)* (44)
MERRYMAN, Martha 17* (B) (28)
MIDDLETON, Catherine 47, Luticia 15, Julia 11 (17)
MIDDLETON, David W. 19, Aslee B. 21 (23)
MIDDLETON, Jackson 18* (23)
MIDDLETON, Jos. 51, Jane 43, Eliza 19, Daniel 14, Martha J. 8, Mary 4, James 11, Maggie 9 (22)
MIDDLETON, Mary E. 20* (22)
MIDDLETON, Solomon 50 (B), Judia 59, Dinah 101 (21)
MIDDLETON, William 15* (24)
MILAM, Wm. Henry 52*, M. A. 50 (f), Nancy E. 23, Darthula 20, Frances F. 17, William G. 19, Dolly 15, R. C. 13 (f), M. J. 11 (f), Etta 9, Jas. H. 6 (51)

MILLER, Abram 30, Ruth 30, Elizabeth 3, Sallie 1 (19)
MILLER, D. 25 (m), M. 24 (f), J. T.? 5 (m), M. B. 4 (f), J. S. 2 (m) (66)
MILLER, E. M. 19 (m), E. A. 19 (f), Sarah 1 (63)
MILLER, Eaphrum 25*, Mary 23, Margarett R. 6/12 (93)
MILLER, Eliza 57*, Sarah 20 (90)
MILLER, Elizabeth 48*, Charles 17, Hattie A. 11 (93)
MILLER, J. P. 27 (m), M. 21 (f) (71)
MILLER, J. R. 48 (m), Nancy M. 26, Eliza J. 15, Moriah F. 14, Janette? 12, Julia 10, Pricilla 8, Thos. E. 3, Columbus 1 (91)
MILLER, Kelly 23, Elizabeth 23 (88)
MILLER, M. 52 (f), Pendleton 26, Sren? 24 (m), Charley 23, M. J. 21? (f), G. A. 3 (m), F. 7/12 (m) (66)
MILLER, M. O. 34 (m), M. F. 31 (f), M. F. 11? (f), W. G. 8 (m), L. C. 6 (f), L. L. 4 (f) (71)
MILLER, Martha L. 23* (26)
MILLER, Monro 34*, Bettie 46, Isabell 40, Rachal 37, Escker? 12 (m), Catharine 6 (93)
MILLER, R. 60 (f)* (66)
MILLER, R. C. 22 (m), Sarah 25, W. E. 4 (m), S. L. 1 (m), R. C. 2/12 (m), Nancy 60 (66)
MILLER, T. J. 75 (m), T. E. 50 (f), J. N. 16 (m), J. I.? 15 (m), M. F. 14 (f), C. H. 10 (m), H. E. 8 (m), D. S. 5 (m) (63)
MILLER, T. M. 44 (m), Mildred 40, J. M. 15 (m), E. B. 14 (m), M. S. 9 (m), A. F. 5 (m) (61)
MILLER, T.? 40 (m)* (68)
MILLER, W. C. 33 (m)*, M. F. 32 (f), D. A. 11 (f), A. J. 4 (m), A. H. 1 (m) (63)
MILLER, W. G. 37 (m), S. H. 24 (f), B. G. 5 (f), S. A. 4 (f), M. E. 3 (f), W. H. 1 (m) (66)
MILLER, W. T. 38 (m), C. K. 40 (f), D. 18 (f), H. T. 12 (m), H. A. 9 (f), D. A. 7 (f) (67)
MILLER, William C. 39*, Frances J. 40, Tennessee E. 10, John W. 9, Leroy M. 6, Charles T. 5 (15)
MILLNER, William 23, Sallie 18, Mary C. 3/12 (5)
MILLS, Benjn. 40, D. C. 34 (f), S. E. 14 (f), M. F. 11 (f), A. A 10 (f), J. W. 8 (m), F. A. 6 (f), N. M. 4 (f), A. J. 2/12 (47)
MILLS, George 36, Bloda? 39 (f), Houston 18 (86)
MILLS, Tilman 43, Elizabeth 30, B. G. 13 (m), M. M. 7 (f), Wm. J. 4, Jno. H. 1 (48)
MILTON, Wilson B. 58, Mehala C. 41, Wilson H. 9, William J. 7, Arga E. 4 (37)
MINURVY, James T. 52, John T. 21, Jeferson D. 18, George W. 16, Martin 14, William 12, Catharine 10, Elisabeth 10, Warden 7 (38)
MITCHEL, Elisabeth 43*, William 16, Mary 14, Fanny 11, Carley 3 (39)
MITCHELL, Richard 20* (B) (20)
MONGOMREY, J. C. 47 (m), L. M. 22 (f), M. E. 3 (f), T. A. 1 (f) (82)
MONTAGUE, Abram 29 (B), Caroline 21, Clarance 5, Milton 3, Mary 1, Abe Lincoln 16 (27)
MONTAGUE, Robt. 14* (B) (21)
MONTAGUE, Squire 50* (B), Tempa 60 (30)
MONTGOMERY, Hugh F. 25*, Mary A. 58, Huldah 23 (13)
MONTGOMERY, Jack 38* (B), Mary 26, Charles W. 9, Nancy A. 6, Lucy E. 5, James W. 2, John A. 3/12 (26)
MONTGOMERY, James 27* (B), Catharine 30, Ann 22, Mary B. 5, Frances A. 3, Jane 1 (25)
MONTGOMERY, James G. 53, Pirthena E. 47, Adaline 23, Jesse L. 21 (13)
MONTGOMERY, James H. 27, Frances A. 26, Cora E. 3, Robert L. 2 (14)

MONTGOMERY, John J. 36, Sarah M. 39, Frances E. 16, Sarah A. 13, Marion J. N. 8, Mary M. 3 (13)
MONTGOMERY, Robert J. 25, Martha M. A. 20, Nora E. 1 (13)
MONTGOMERY, Robert J. 39, Margaret 43, Buel J. 18, Mary A. 16, Francis M. 13, Leander L. 10, Robert H. 8, Sarilda C. 5 (8)
MONTGOMERY, William J. 38, Mary R. 46, Martha J. 13, Hugh B. 7, Rosa D. 3 (14)
MONTGOMERY, William W. 74, Susan 54, Almarene 15, Tennessee A. 13, Joseph W. 9 (14)
MOODY, Asa T. 32*, Nancy L. 34, Walter P. 7, Frances E. 5, James L. 1 (38)
MOODY, Catharine 34* (19)
MOODY, Enos 62*, Elender 59, Mahalia E. 27, Enos W. 23 (54)
MOODY, Polly 65 (36)
MOODY, Solomon 13* (B), Caladona 11, Esther 9 (17)
MOODY, Stephen A. 27, Elisabeth E. 25, William W. 7, Sarah E. 5, James H. 2 (36)
MOODY, William H. 37, Sarah E. 41 (36)
MOORE, A. 13 (m)* (74)
MOORE, A. J. 38 (m)*, F. E. 22 (f), S. M. 8 (f) (44)
MOORE, A. L. 64 (m)*, Charity 54, J. M. 16 (m), E. J. 12 (f) (74)
MOORE, B. 49 (m), S. A. 50 (f), M. 25 (f), S. E. 22 (f), W. T. 20 (m), C.? 18 (m), J. J. 14 (m), B. J. 14 (f), John 12, M. J. 11 (f), H. A. 7 (f), W. J. 5 (m) (74)
MOORE, B. W. 51 (m), B. 44 (f), B. L. 18 (m), L. T. 17 (m), J. T. 14 (m), J. H. 10 (m), F. J. 9 (f), P. C. 6 (m), J. V. 4 (m), G. H. 1 (m) (76)
MOORE, E. 61 (f)* (83)
MOORE, Elam 50, Mary M. 40, Catherine R. 9 (42)
MOORE, G. E. 19 (m), M. A. 16 (f) (63)
MOORE, George 18* (23)
MOORE, Henry 28*, M. E. 27 (f) (43)
MOORE, J. H. 10 (m)* (78)
MOORE, John 26*, Elizabeth 23, James 5, Wm. F. 3, G. Pleasant 9/12 (48)
MOORE, L. 15 (f)* (75)
MOORE, Louey? P. 50, Wm. G. 17, Jas. G. 14, Margret Z. 12, Jesse F. 9, Leroy G. 7, Elijah S. 3 (44)
MOORE, T. J. 22 (m), M. A. 23 (f) (77)
MORAN, Wesley 29, Louisa 33, Bobera? 2 (f), Emma L. 3/12 (23)
MORELAND, Saml. 84*, Jane 70 (48)
MORELAND, Saml. W. 24*, Eliza J. 21, Prudy 59, William 31 (56)
MORGAIN, Dunken 28*, C. J. 25 (f), L. S.? 5 (m), Geo. S. 3, J. ?. 1 (m), E. E. 52 (f) (60)
MORGAN, G. M. 39 (m)*, M. A. 37 (f), Rachel 9, N. A. 7 (m), G. A. 3 (m), L. A. 2/12 (f) (48)
MORGAN, George 75, Mollie 75, Viana 43 (7)
MORGAN, James W. 46*, Martha M. 38, George W. 18, James 11, John F. 10, Andrew 4 (6)
MORGAN, John L. 53, Martha C. 52, Cordelia 22, Emily 13, William 10 (14)
MORGAN, Martha D.? 39, Enoch S. 18, Mary S. 16, Ollie J. 11 (f), Salina E. 9 (12)
MORGAN, Polly J. 28*, John 7, Racheal J.? 5, James A. 1 (12)
MORGAN, William 33, Eliza 29 (29)
MORRIS, Alla 24 (m), Lavena 27, Wm. A. 1 (88)
MORRIS, Benj. F. 39, Roena J. 38, Mary E. J. 14, Sary C. 6, Lydia M. 3, Robert F. 2/12 (4)
MORRIS, Benjamin 78, Hariet J. 34, Solomon S. 16, Lydia E. 13, George W.? 10, Tennessee

J. 8, Emily 5 (3)
MORRIS, Charles J. 23, Mary A. 24, unnamed 11/12 (m) (1)
MORRIS, Dolly A. 51?, John A. 20?, Nancy J. 17 (88)
MORRIS, James 32, Emeline 31, W. T.? 6 (m), Lusadore 2, Leona 4/12 (88)
MORRIS, L. C. 22 (m), Mary E. 23, Ola J. 3 (52)
MORRIS, William 49* (25)
MURPHEY, Franklin M. 31, Eliza J. 37, Lucinda 8, Mary E. 6, Sary A. 3 (2)
MURPHEY, John T. 42, Mary A. 38, Charles 9, Mary L. 7, Martha E. 6, Robert 3, Daniel L. 2, John H. 8/12 (2)
MURPHEY, Luisa D. 50, Martha A. 22 (2)
MURPHY, Amanda 39, Tennessee 13, Mark 12, Emma 5 (34)
MURPHY, C. Jarrot? 41*, P. Jane 37, F. Mary 13, O. Almar 11, G. Grant 8, M. Cordelia 5, M. Jane 5/12 (51)
MURPHY, Calvin B. 49*, Mary E. 37, John 11, Anna 69 (57)
MURPHY, Martha 7James W.*, Alsa A. 21, Isaac 18, Milton A. 29, Martha D. 25, James N. 6, Martha E. 4, Thena A. 8/12 (24)
MURPHY, William 35 (B), Jane 26, William 20, John 18, Mary 14, Jessee 13, Alfred 9 (27)
MURPHY, William A. 43, Frances E. 34, Mary L. 13, Emma E. 11, Sarah L.? 9, Martha C. 7, John W. 5, Jinnie F. 7/12, Elizabeth 60 (25)
MURPY, William 19, Margurete 20, Ella 1 (34)
MYERS, Freeman 21, Rilda A. 20, William 2 (22)
MYRACLE, B. W. 26 (m), C. P. 28 (f), L. A. 1 (f) (45)
MYRACLE, B. W. 58 (m), M. A. 51 (f) (80)
MYRACLE, H. 60 (m)*, J. A. 22 (m), M. C. 18 (m) (82)
MYRACLE, H. W. 41 (m), Nancy 25, J. W. 11 (m), C. J. 7 (f) (80)
MYRACLE, J. C. P. 43 (m)*, M. A. 34 (f), L. W. C. 8 (m), A. J. 5 (f), J. I. 2 (f), J. F. 8/12 (m) (80)
MYRACLE, L. L. 68 (m), J. H. 62 (f), M. J. 19 (f) (80)
MYRACLE, L. W. 20 (m)* (80)
MYRACLE, W. A. 23 (m)*, Barbra 49, Justine 16, Louvina 8, Mary E. 6, Maggie 2 (45)
NALES?, W. R. 22 (m), Judy A. 23, H. A. 4 (f), Jophine 2, J. G. 11/12 (m) (60)
NEALL, James V. 25*, Margarett J. 20 (26)
NEELY, H. B. 25 (m)* (56)
NEWMAN, Bird S. 46*, Lucy A. 44, Mary J. 12, Robert L. 11, Molly S. 9, Maddon F. 9, Minnie E. 1 (14)
NEWSOM, Green 38, Rachal C. 37, Martha E. 14, Lucy J. 12, Daniel 9, John H. 7, Monro 5, Elbert 3, Joseph 1 (91)
NEWSOM, Joseph 59, Sopha 52, Matilda 24, T. A. 21 (f) (44)
NEWSOM, P. 54? (f), Wm. 25, John 22, Joseph 20, Charles 18 (91)
NEWSOM, W. 38 (m), Ann 35, Cassie 14, Thos. 11, Proktar 8 (87)
NEWSON, J. O. 48 (m), Harrett 36, Robert 16, Wm. S. 14, M. F. 11 (f), Joseph D. 8, George W. 4, Gillum 2 (89)
NIBLETT, Robt. 20* (86)
NICHOLAS, Wm. 57, Mary A. 55, Robert 16, Julia A. 13 (92)
NICHOLS, Elio? 8 (m)* (25)
NICHOLS, Emma E. 28* (20)
NUNLEY, Sidney 8*, M. D. 7 (f) (61)
NURSE, Charles 54* (B), Anjaline 32 (21)

OAKLEY, C. P. 26 (m)* (20)
OAKLEY, Sarah 10* (27)
OAKLEY, Thomas 24* (20)
OAKLEY, Upton 67* (19)
ODLE, D. R. 38 (m)*, Eliza 30, Emma F. 11, Columbus W. 10, Arther J. 8, Albert A. 6, James J. 5, Perry R. 2, Joseph E. 10/12 (90)
ODLE, Dick 44* (90)
ODLE, J. R. 29 (m)*, Debora 31, A. E. 1 (f) (81)
ODLE, J. R. 64 (m)*, Lucy 34 (87)
ODLE, Samp 31*, Sallie 21, Frances Gray 5, Lucy E. 3, Avner 3/12 (m) (90)
OGLE, John 52, Nancy A. 48, Samuel 21, John R. 18, Gemima 17, Rebeca F. 9, Mary L. 6 (11)
ONEAL, Dennis H. 48, Elizabeth M. 48, Martha 22, Benjamin F. 20, John R. J. 15, Margaret M. 13 (8)
ONEAL, Fanny 30*, Cintha A. 9, Adda F. 2 (2)
ONEAL, James 27, Mary 20 (50)
ONEAL, Thos. 65, L. M. 65 (f) (50)
ORE, William C. 26, Emily A. 19 (13)
ORR, Georg 25* (29)
OSHER?, Bes. 30 (f)* (92)
OWENSBY, Margurete 36, Sarah A. 10, John T. 9, Mary E. 7 (34)
PALMER, William 47, Permela A. 41, Sarah F. 18, Serrena M. 10, Elisabeth 6, Larcena 3 (37)
PAROTT, William 10* (B) (56)
PARRISH, J. W. 21 (m)* (B), M. J. 24 (f), J. H. W. 3 (m), P. R. 2 (f) (82)
PARROTT, Rutha A. 60* (B) (56)
PARSON, J. 27 (f) (B), N. 10 (m), E. 8 (m), J. A. 4 (f), M. 2 (f) (70)
PARSON, Mary 20* (B) (56)
PARSONS, Bogue? 20 (B), Mary A. 16 (56)
PARSONS, Elen 26 (B), L. E. 6 (f), R. M. 3 (f), M. A. 3 (f), J. E. 1 (f) (62)
PARSONS, Gilbert 22* (B) (53)
PARSONS, L. E. 5 (f)* (B) (69)
PARSONS, Luth 40 (f) (B), Andrew 17, M. E. 11 (f) (62)
PARSONS, Pleas 17* (B) (56)
PARSONS, R. 55 (f)* (B) (74)
PARSONS, T.? 22 (f) (B), C. 8 (f), Bass 3 (66)
PARSONS, W. 35 (m) (B), R. J. 40 (f), N. L. 10 (m), O. W. 4 (m) (62)
PARSONS, William 20* (B) (56)
PARTIN, G. W. 23 (m)* (77)
PATE, A. 22 (f)* (69)
PATE, K. N. 54 (m), P. 45 (f), M. M. 24 (f), N. J. 18 (m), J. T. 13 (m), K. 12 (f), V. 10 (f), S. 8 (m), M. Z.? 1 (m) (69)
PATE, Mary E. 44, Abi 8 (f) (38)
PATE, Nancy 52, Frances 19, Troy E. 17, Nancy F. 14 (38)
PATE, Samuel H. 25, Rebecca J. 31, Marcus D. L. 5, Hetty E. 3 (37)
PATRICK, W. M. 35 (m), C. S. 30 (f), A. 9 (m) (69)
PATTERSON, Isah 35, Jennettee 32, Emily E. 13, Robert H. 11, Stephen W. 8, James B. 6, Matilda L. 4, Cami? 8/12 (f), Lucinda 78 (31)

PATTERSON, Isaih M. 32, Margaret J. 31, Sarah J. 11, William C. 8, John L . 4, Nancy E. 1 (14)
PATTERSON, James R. 48, David H. 16, Josiah 8, James R. 5, John R. 2 (38)
PATTERSON, John C. 24, Margaret M.A.C.21, Lilly 4, Arra E. 10/12 (8)
PATTERSON, John S. 55, Martha A. 30, Benjamin 5, Perry A. 1 (f), Frances A. 13, Lucinda 77 (8)
PATTERSON, William F. 27*, Sarah Jane 23, Margurite A. 4, James T. 2, William F. 6/12 (38)
PATTERSON?, Samuel S. 7* (29)
PATTON, Paul E. 49, Martha E. 25, James W. 17, John S.? 16, Nancy J. 13, Benjamin 10, Isaac S. 8, George C. 7, Frances A. 5, Mary 1 (28)
PEARCY, J. H. 70 (m)*, Lavina 49, Holley 10 (m), Oliver 6 (46)
PEARSON, Elizabeth 53, William M. 25, John F. 23, Perry A. 21, Sarah E. 17, Francis A. 15, Richard 13, David 9, Ellen 11 (22)
PEARSON, James H. 27* (20)
PEARSON, K. H. 61 (m)*, Rebecca 44, G. W. 18? (m), Luticia 16, Malissa 14 (47)
PEARSON, Mitchel 48, Mary A. 31, Mitty 5 (36)
PERRY, John 31, F. M. 21 (f), S. J. 1 (f) (77)
PERRY, M. 71 (f), M. A. 39 (f), J. A. 17 (f) (79)
PERRY, William F. 27, Mary E. 31, William J. 2 (58)
PERY, James 24, Mar;y 29, William 1, Frank 8/12, Martha J. 52 (20)
PERY, John 15* (20)
PETIGREW, Elisha 23* (B), Kizzy 24, Matuson 5, Cela L. 2, Mollie? J. 4/12 (25)
PETTEGREW, J. K.? 36 (m)*, M. A. 27 (f), C. P. 8 (f), L. B. 5 (f), M. M. 3 (f), L. H. 1 (f) (83)
PETTIGREW, B. 64 (m) (B), Martha 45, Washington 14, Mo? 11 (f), Harrison 9, Ben 8, P. M. 4 (m) (78)
PETTIGREW, C. 40 (f) (B), L. 16 (f), F. 15 (m), L. 12 (m), L. 10 (f), W. 8 (m), F. 7 (f), C. 4 (m) (75)
PETTIGREW, C. 68 (m) (B), B. 55 (f), H. 17 (m), D. 14 (m) (83)
PETTIGREW, F. S. 78 (m) (B), Caroline 70, C. H. 17 (f) (78)
PETTIGREW, George W. 43 (B), Maria J. 28, James 10, William 6, Milford 4, Mary A. 3, Ader 6/12 (55)
PETTIGREW, Gracy 59* (B) (53)
PETTIGREW, J. F. 18 (m)* (B) (74)
PETTIGREW, Jo 23 (m) (B), M. 19 (f), J. A. 5/12 (m) (75)
PETTIGREW, John 26 (B), L. 21 (f), J. W. 3 (m), Samuel 2, Jerry 2/2? (74)
PETTIGREW, John C. 33 (B), Cassa A. 37, Martha J. 9, William A. 5, Charley L. 4, Anner E. 4/12 (55)
PETTIGREW, Leander 52 (B), Ann 32, John 14, Henry 11, Dee 10 (m), Jessee 8, Hervy 4, Levine? 8/12 (40)
PETTIGREW, Thomas J. 39*, Mary A. 58, Ella M. 10, Corry H. 7 (m), Martha A. 5, Elizabeth C. 2 (54)
PETTIGREW, William 47 (B), Chloe 37, Correy 19 (m), Edwin 13, Billey 6 (f), George 4, Anna 2 (57)
PETTIGREW, Zilpha 60* (B) (55)
PETTY, J. M. 24 (m)*, Nanny 22, M. B. 9/12 (m), T. M. 22 (m) (62)
PETTY, Jane 40*, George 12, Mollie 7?, Willie 1 (93)

PETTY, S. E. 23 (f)* (63)
PETTY, W. A. C. 51 (m), S. A. 23 (f), W. H. 4 (m) (62)
PETTYGREW, A. 20 (m)* (B) (62)
PHILIPS, Elizabeth 78* (19)
PHILLIPS, A. J. 29 (m), Louisa E. 23, James S. 2, William N. 3/12 (19)
PICKENS, Ann 17* (B) (51)
PIERCY?, M. L. 19 (m)* (77)
PITMAN, Mary 40*, Ellin 11 (36)
PITMAN, Mary 40* (52)
PITMAN, Susan 19* (44)
PITT, M. 10 (f)* (B) (76)
PITTMAN, Anna 15* (10)
PITTS, A. 12 (f)* (B) (78)
PITTS, Leah 55 (B), Harriett 19 (20)
PITTS, Levi 18*, Ed 4, John 30, Jane 25, M. J. 5 (f) (90)
PITTS, Sarah 22* (B), Amanda 6, Will 4, Ella 2 (53)
PITTS, William N. 37, Isabell A. 37, William A. 14, Vanburen 12, George W. 10, James H. 8, Mary M. 6, John W. 5, Martin L. 2, Mary A. 57 (29)
POOR, John 34*, Almina 7 (23)
POOR, Mary 35, Daniel 13, William H. 8 (39)
POPE, Henry 31* (40)
PORE?, Mary 33*, Nancy 7 (58)
PORTERFIELD, James M. 41, Mary E. 31, Reeder W. 9, Lillian 8, Matty E. 6, James 5, Lewis 3, Edwin Lee 1, Robert A. 1/12 (57)
POWERS, John 15* (50)
PRATT, Betty 50, Angeline 21, Jno. W. 16 (48)
PRATT, J. H. 37 (m), M. E. 29 (f), Lilly 9, R. G. 8 (m), J. W. 6 (m), E. L. 4 (m), D. V. 2 (f) (64)
PRATT, James M. 34, Nancy J. 34, James A. 11, Amand? 9, Eliza E. 6, Caldona J. 3, William F. 1, Emeline 53 (5)
PRATT, P. S. 28 (m)*, W. J. 25 (f), O. T. 6 (m), G. M. 3 (m), W. E. 1 (m), N. A. 25 (m) (62)
PRATT, R. J. 22 (m)* (63)
PRATT, W. J. 25 (m), Elizabeth 24, M. A. 5 (f), Prudy 3, Eliza 2, Martha 2/12 (48)
PRATT, William 52, Mary J. 36, Kittura E. 20, John W. 18, Noah J. 9 (58)
PRESLAR, Margarett 14* (1)
PRICE, James 47, Susan 46, Sidney 10, Claudius 6 (85)
PRICE, James D. 26*, Sarah C. 36, Sarah E. 6, Louisa C. 6, Nancy A. 2 (38)
PRICE, Nancy 38*, Mary A. 15, Darthula 7 (29)
PRICE, Riley 21*, Mary 22 (93)
PRICE, Robert C. 48, Margarett 43, Martha A. 18, Robert Z. 9, Harvey L. 6, Hannah M. 69 (29)
PRIM, B. G. 23 (m)*, Mattie 16 (f) (65)
PRIM, C. 25 (f)* (63)
PRINCE, E. 32 (m)*, Frankie 33 (f), Welbie? 4 (m), _____ 2 (m) (93)
PRITCHARD, R. 73 (f), Nancy 30 (69)
PRITCHARD, William 68*, Mary 68 (51)
PRITCHETT, Elijah 67, Eliza 52, Rachel 22, Oren 18, Mary A. 15, Elijah 12, Thomas 10, George 6, John 4 (29)

QUILLIN, Frances 30*, Clara T. 8 (20)
QUINN, Abb 48, L. 46 (f), P. 21 (f), J. 19 (m), E. 17 (m), M. J. 14 (f), Lee 11 (m), B. S. 8 (f), B. 6 (f) (66)
QUINN, G. 22 (m), I. B. 16 (f), J. 4/12 (m) (72)
QUINN, J. 33 (m), Mary 23, A. M. 5 (m), C.L.S. 1/12? (m) (68)
QUINN, J. C. 16 (m)* (67)
QUINN, J. M. 40 (m), M. P. 39 (f), unnamed 1/30 (f) (69)
QUINN, N. 34 (f)* (69)
QUINN, P. 38 (m), Jane 28 (66)
QUINN, R. J. 42 (f), S. A. 18 (f) (72)
QUINN, R. M. 44 (m), M. 42 (f), C. W. 20 (m), J. T. 18 (m), J. 16 (m), F. 14 (m), M. L. 8 (f), P. 6 (f), J. 3 (m), E. 4/12 (m) (68)
RAINES, J. 45 (m), S. J. 48 (f), W. 21 (m), J. M. 19 (m), J. W. 13 (m) (70)
RAINS, B. 78 (m), Matilda 68 (82)
RAINS, E. 42 (f)* (B), E. 2 (m), C. J. 3/12 (m), Samuel 14 (83)
RAINS, H. H. 39? (m), M. J. 31 (f), J. P.? 13 (m), J. D. 10 (m) (70)
RAINS, John P. 47, Rebecca J. 26, Lena 7, John H. 5 (57)
RAINS, M. 34 (f)* (B), R. 10 (m), B. 8 (f), D. 5 (f) (74)
RAINS, R. Z. 53 (m)*, S. J. 54 (f), L. A. 10 (m) (77)
RAINS, S. 30 (f)* (B), Dora 5, Will 3, Fletcher 4/12 (83)
RAINS, Sam 40* (B), Elizabeth 47 (60)
RAINS, Venus 22 (f)* (B), Ida 4, William 3/12 (82)
RAINS, W. Guston? 42*, Joan 32, Ethel 9, William G. 3 (57)
RAINS, W. M. 21 (m)* (75)
RAINS, W. P. 41 (m), E. A. 30 (f), M. L. 12 (f), A. L. 11 (m), M. V. 9 (f), F. E. 7 (f), J. 5 (m), H. 3 (f), W. E. 1 (m) (70)
RAINS?, Bob 23 (B), Liddy 51, Rindy 18 (f), July 16 (f) (40)
RANEY, Bryant W. 28* (41)
RANEY, G. M. 32 (m)*, Lucy 24, Maggie 3, M. Jane 1 (53)
RANEY, Jas. H. sr. 60, Jas. H. jr. 22, J. D. 19 (m), Barbara E. 12 (54)
REAMES, Babe 22 (f)*, Nancy 6, _____ 4 (f), _____ 1 (f) (92)
REAVES, H. B. 33 (m), J. S. 36 (f), S. L. 12 (f), A. 10 (f), R. G. 9 (m), M. J. 6 (f), E. 3 (f) (69)
REDON, John 29, Artlissa 27, Pleasant 10, Alzy 8, Louanora 4, Calla 1 (31)
REED, James 12* (B) (21)
REED, My 26 (m)* (B) (20)
REEVES, C. 46 (m), Emeline 38, Reevis 20 (f), Nancy 16, Sena 13, Tom 9, Jo Donce? 6 (f), Andrew 3 (85)
REID, Isaac 83, Sarah 48, Thos. R. 18, Jas. V. 15, Amanda M. 24 (47)
REMBAR?, A. G. 18 (m)* (75)
RENFRO, William H. 32, Emily 27, M. Joshua 8, John W. 5, Joseph T. 3, George H. 3/12 (16)
RENFROE, Nathaniel 68, Sarah E. 47, Hannah L. 15, Mark 14, Harriett E. 12, Martha P. 11, Mary A. 10, Nathaniel W. 8, Joanna 5, Sophia E. 4, Hannah 66 (25)
RENSHAW, J. W. 38 (m), J. T. 37? (f), C. H. 18 (m), M. E. 17 (f), J. A. 14 (m), J. T. 10 (m), N. J. 8 (f), L. M. 6 (f), M. M. 3 (f), M. 1/12 (f) (71)
REYNOLDS, Caroline 33, Jacob E. 7, Betsy A. 12 (37)
REYNOLDS, John 19* (16)

REYNOLDS, John N. 20" (30)
RHOADS, G. 44 (m), S. C. 47 (f), S. 6 (m), C. A. 1 (m) (75)
RHOADS, J. R. 2 (m)*, S. N. 5/12 (m) (76)
RHOADS, W. T. 44 (m)*, M. J. 27 (f), W. M. 19 (m), J. A. 16 (m), M. C. 12 (f), M. E. 9 (f), G. T. 4 (m) (75)
RICE, Havy? A. 22 (m) (86)
RICE, Henry 11* (B) (26)
RICE, J. C. W. 73 (m)*, Vinie 61? (85)
RICE, J. M. 52 (m)*, E. S.? 36 (f), F. M. 16 (f), S. F. 10 (m), L. E. 8 (f), D. J. 5 (m) (86)
RICE, Jinnie 25* (23)
RICE, Oliver T. 38, Fanny 32, Ider B. 14, Sallie A. 12, Lilie A. 10, George E. 8, Robert 6, Luler E. 11/12 (89)
RICE, V. A. 28 (m)*, Mary A. 22, Maud 2, Claud 3/12 (88)
RICE, Wm. V.? 30, E. F. 30 (f), Sallie 6, John 4, James 2, Lora 6/12 (85)
RICHARDSON, B.? T. 22 (m)* (B) (77)
RICKETTS, Judea 69, Sary 30, Tilman 6 (7)
RIGGS, C. 28 (m), E. J. 20 (f) (80)
RIGGS, J. C. 16 (m), B. A. 10 (m), F. 6 (m) (76)
RIGGS, J. C. 46 (m), M. T. 32 (f), M. A. 16 (f), M. C. 8 (f), S. W. 7 (m), S. M. 3 (m), E. J. 2 (f), infant 1/12 (m) (80)
RIGGS, J. G. 24 (m), M. 23 (f), Dilie? 5, Ednia 2 (67)
RIGGS, J. J. 34 (m), E. C. 39 (f), L. E. 5 (f), J. S. 3 (m) (79)
RIGGS, J. W. 27 (m), M. J. 31 (f), M. A. 10 (m), M. C. 7 (f), R. C. 6 (f) (67)
RIGGS, J. W. 44 (m), R. L. A. 44 (f), M. E. 14 (f) (64)
RIGGS, S. W. 43 (m)*, M. J. 42 (f), W. D. 21 (m), J. T. 19 (m), L. M. 10 (f), Addie 6, D. B. 2 (f), B. E. 1 (f) (67)
RIGGS, W. G. 52 (m), S. E. 47 (f), M. A. 18 (f), R. J. 16 (f), P. L. 10 (m) (68)
RIMER, George W. 30, Tennessee 23, Mary E. 6, Dora A. 1 (7)
RIMER, Martha J. 44* (7)
RIMMER, J. H. 34 (m)* (50)
RIMMER, J. W. 28 (m), Margret 17 (50)
RINGER, Joab 50* (85)
RITTER, Moses 25* (92)
ROACH, Addison L. 37*, Penina I. 30, Emma J. 13, William C. 3 (14)
ROACH, Belzora J. 17*, Thomas 1 (47)
ROACH, Elizabeth 80 (14)
ROAVER, John 3* (B) (19)
ROBERDS, W. T. 26 (m), F. A. 23 (f) (80)
ROBERTS, Amanda 60* (17)
ROBERTS, Ferba J. 26* (21)
ROBERTS, Houston 60, Permelia 51, Betty P. 13 (57)
ROBERTS, J. Monroe 25, M. R. 19 (f), M. E. 2 (f) (50)
ROBERTS, Mahalia 49*, Perlina 18, James L. 13 (43)
ROBERTS, P. Franklin 28, Virgnia 29, Ida 1, Inezie 1 (51)
ROBERTS, Pinkney O. 34, Laura 27, Albert C. 10, Clara G. 8, Fanny L. 6, Maude E. 4, Alace M. 1 (58)
ROBERTS, Squire 32*, G. E. 27 (f), Jesse L. 10, Permelia A. 7, Susana 2, Noland 1 (51)
ROBERTS, W. 23 (m)* (63)

ROBINSON, James 55, Deba J. 54 (43)
ROCHELL, William T. 30, Elizabeth 26, James F. 10, Mary L. C. 6, Martha D. E. 4, Robert R. 2, John W. P. 10/12 (7)
RODEN, Frank 67* (86)
ROGERS, J. Tate 38, Fredonia A. 17, Charles 11/365 (56)
ROGERS, Jefferson D. 18* (5)
ROGERS, M. 63 (f), M. C. 31 (f), M. C. 16 (f) (82)
ROGERS, Sarah J. 40*, Jackson 19 (56)
ROLIDA?, Benson 60*, Lucinda 56, Parallel E. 20, Julia 17 (30)
RONE, Fredona 25*, George 4, Coraann 2 (35)
RONE, Joseph T. 6* (36)
ROSE, Charley 13* (B) (56)
ROSS, Charles 25 (B), Ellen 26, Thomas 5 (23)
ROSSON, J. 44 (m)*, E. 45 (f), J. F. 13 (m), M. F. 9 (f), D. 18 (f) (82)
ROSSON, John 73, Nancy 74, N. J. 38 (f), L. L. 14 (m), J. F. 13 (m), C. M. 7 (f), N. H. 5 (f), W. J. 2 (m) (79)
ROSSON, L. T. 51 (m), M. E. 45 (f), Isabell 15, J. A. 12 (m), Bettie 10 (80)
ROSSON, P. J. 21 (f)* (80)
ROUQUIEM?, Henry 19* (B) (85)
ROUSA, Rebeca 30* (5)
ROWZY?, James D. 23* (32)
RUDDLE, John 30, C. R. 9 (f). M. C. 7 (f), Sarah A. 16, T. L. 21 (f) (48)
RUFF, Allen 15* (86)
RUFF, Elbert 10* (88)
RUSHING, Clinton 35, Louisa 37, Sarah J. 19, Elizabeth 11, James C. 10, John W. 8, Dickson 6, Dorah A. 3, Sidney 1 (24)
RUSHING, E. Dees 27 (m), M. T. 20 (f) (44)
RUSHING, Eliza 62, Milard 27, S. L. R. 17 (f), W. B. 24 (m), Jane 22 (46)
RUSHING, Elizabeth 36, S. H. 16 (m), D.? J. 11 (f), S. E. 5 (f) (50)
RUSHING, G. B. 31 (m)*, Laura 24, A. L. 4 (f), G. L. 1 (m) (49)
RUSHING, J. L. 30 (m), S. A. 29 (f), W. E. 8 (m), S. 5 (f), L. 1/12 (f) (75)
RUSHING, J. Wesley 29*, M. A. 23 (f), L. A. 5 (f), B. F. 3 (m), A. E. 10/12 (f) (47)
RUSHING, Joel 73*, Lucy 59 (45)
RUSHING, John 29, L. J. 23 (f), A. E. 3 (f), E. G. 7/12 (m) (46)
RUSHING, Lee 42, M. J. 30 (f), James 10, Sophia 9, Minnie 8, Eliza 6, Etter 4, Wm. 1 (44)
RUSHING, M. 40 (f), L. F. 11 (f), J. M. 7 (m) (70)
RUSHING, N. A. 39? (f), Wm. F. 12, M. F. 10 (m), C. O. 8 (f), J. R. 5 (m), W. C. 3 (f), Ella J. 4/12 (45)
RUSHING, R. B. 52 (m)*, Mary J. 38, A.J.L.J. 11 (f), Wm. 7, M. L. 4 (f), J. F. 3 (m) (47)
RUSHING, W. F. 43 (m)*, S. A. 41 (f) (50)
RUSHING, W. H. H. 42 (m)*, E. A. 31 (f), Nancy J. 6, Cora M. 1 (44)
RUSHING, Wm. T. 42*, Martha ;32, J. G. 10 (m), Jason W. 8, Wm. F. 5, Roxyanna 8/12 (44)
RUSSELL, Elizabeth 67* (47)
RUSSELL, James 49, Anthum? 34 (f), Jno. W. 14, S. E. 7 (f), F. E. 4 (f), V. V. 11/12 (f) (51)
RUSSELL, Mary A. 25* (31)
RUSSELL, T. J. 62 (m), M. E. 51 (f), H. P. 22 (m), A. F. 14 (f) (79)
RUSSELL, William H. 24, Nancy W. 22, James B. 5, William H.? 2, John A. 2/12 (31)

SAFFORD, W. L. 52 (m)*, M. J. 44 (f), J. C. 21 (f), I. D. 18 (m), J. W. 16 (m), S. C. 13 (f), J. N. 10 (m), T. A. 9 (m), M. J. 7 (f) (77)
SAINT, George W. 21* (36)
SAINT, H. A. 33 (m), Catherine 30, John 6, William 4, Zora 1 (48)
SAINT, Hosea 54*, C. C. 34 (f), George 24, Catherine 9 (49)
SANDERS, James 28* (B), Ida 23, Elija 8, Mary F. 7, Emmer L. 5, Ulysis 3, Adilee 6/12 (21)
SANDERS, Jessee 16* (B) (29)
SAVAGE, A. C. 39 (f)* (50)
SAVAGE, Henry 25, Martha J. 25, M. L. 4 (f), Jas. W. 2, Ella J. 6/12 (51)
SAVAGE, James 39, Nancy 30, Mary J. 12, Sarah C. 11, James M. 9, Martha L. 7, John T. 5, George 2, Liza O. 3/12 (12)
SAVAGE, Jessee P. 21, Parthena 16, Perry C. 9/12 (6)
SAVAGE, William 81, Winny 60, Elijah L. 17, Robert A. 16 (7)
SCIPWORTH, J. 26 (m)*, A. 18 (f), J. A. 2 (m), S. B. 8/12 (m) (76)
SCOTT, Abb 52 (B), Margrett 42, Lucy 18, Wesley 14, James 10, Ellen 8, Henrietta 6, Mat 4, Walter 2, Mary M. 3/12, Minnie L. 3 (52)
SCOTT, Allen 28* (B), Lizza 30, Henrietta 10, Wesley C. 8 (59)
SCOTT, Caroline 32 (B), Lee 14, Sam 10, George 7, John 4, Jasper 2, Thomas 2/12 (55)
SCOTT, David E. 30, Martha E. 29, Frances U.? 1, David M. 63, William S. 28, Nancy 80 (59)
SCOTT, Eddy 18* (B), George 22 (55)
SCOTT, Gabriel 62, Piety 66 (5)
SCOTT, Jane 21 (B), Hubert 3, Tula? 2, Sam C. 7/12 (53)
SCOTT, Jeptha D. 40, Louisa 43 (5)
SCOTT, John V. R. 20, Lucinda E. 24 (5)
SCOTT, Jordan 20* (B) (56)
SCOTT, Joseph 33, Laura 22, Carson A. 3, Amon L. 2 (54)
SCOTT, Luciun 27, Catharine 34, Margarett 28, Sallie 22, John 13 (19)
SCOTT, Martha 23* (B) (53)
SCOTT, Mary 23* (B), William E. 4 (54)
SCOTT, Matilda 55 (B), Cas 20 (f) (53)
SCOTT, Nathan S. 33, Armelia A. 28, Columbus M. 6, Bettie A. 4, Mary E. 2 (2)
SCOTT, Newton 32* (B) (56)
SCOTT, Wilie 66, Belinda C. 40, Eliza J. 31, Eliza A. 15, Jesse B. 14, Jephtha R. 12, Absolom M. 9, Cintha F. 7, John E. O. 3, Allis A. 7/12 (2)
SCOTT, Will 12* (B) (52)
SCOTT, William 43, Piety 42, Jesse R. 20, Cintha E. 16, Lucinda E. 14, Jepthah R. 11, Tennessee 7, John C. 6, Addie 2 (1)
SCOTT, Willis 53 (B), Ida 18, Alace 14, Milton 16, Florence 14 (55)
SEABOLT, James P. 33, Alverett O. 10, Mary M. 9, Rebecca 6, Laentine 3, Prissilla 4/30 (20)
SEABOLT, Robert W. 20, Julia 22 (28)
SEABOLT, Thos. W. 18, Louisa J. 26, Frances H. 23 (20)
SESSUM, Fillmore 28 (B), Harrett 20, William 6, Ida 3 (33)
SHANNON, Alfred 21 (B), Anner 17 (21)
SHANNON, John 23* (21)
SHANNON, John 30* (B), Jane 22, Mary 5, Laura 2, George 2/12 (27)
SHANNON, Lewis 53* (B), Nancy 55, Henry 20, Ann 17, Ida 13, Mariah 14, John 11, Mary

9 (21)
SHANNON, Mark 21 (B), Mary 16 (31)
SHANNON, Mary 20* (B) (31)
SHANNON, Robt. 64*, Mary 56, John R. 30 (25)
SHANNON, Thomas J. 73*, Millie 79 (21)
SHANNON, Thos. S. 69, Margarett 47, Sarah 18, Mary 16, Ader 12, William 8, Mitchell 4, Thomas 31 (31)
SHANNON, Wiley 55 (B), Marry 50, Anderson 14, Lawson 13, Ida 12, William 10 (20)
SHANNON, William 38, Lucinda 36, John T. 12, Mary F. 10, Arby 9 (f), Albert 8, Daisy U. 6, Lucy V. 5, Nathan C. 2, Della 1 (31)
SHANNON, Zilpha 70 (B) (3)
SHARMON, James 20 (B), Ann 22, W. H. 1 (m) (60)
SHARP, Clay 30 (B), Emily 25, Mary 9, Della 6, Marshall 4, Dena 3, John 10/12 (30)
SHEARMAN, S. 57 (m)*, S. T. 36 (f) (72)
SHEBBY?, Charles 28* (31)
SHELTON, Charles 50* (B), Puss 40, John 14, Eddy? 11, Ida J. 4, Leonard 6, Cathaline 3 (56)
SHOEMAKER, M. 76 (f)* (70)
SHOOK, L. D. 38 (m), Martha J. 27, Wm. R. 12, Henry 10, John A. 9, Sarah V. 6, Mollie 2, Flora 3/12 (85)
SIKES, Geo. W. 35, M. E. 24 (f), L. E. 6 (f), R. L. 5 (m), E. O. 11/12 (f) (45)
SIMMONS, Benjamin 26*, Ellen 27, Edgar G. 3/30 (30)
SIMMONS, James R. 24, Marion? 23 (f), John C. 1 (29)
SIMMONS, Prince 30 (B), Laura 24, Bell 6 (f), Mary 4, Eden 2, Esteler 2/12 (27)
SIMMONS, Troy 52*, Saphrona 54, George C. 19, Saphrona A. 21, Carroll H. 18 (16)
SIMMS, William F. 39, Margarett F. 25, Rebecca A. 12, Sarah J. 11, James R. 9, Robt. T. 1, Willam H. 7/12 (30)
SIMPSON, J. P. 35 (m), M. 31 (f), L. E. 13 (f), M. A. 10 (f), L. 3 (f), E. A. 1 (m) (75)
SIMPSON, Marquis F. 46, Elisabeth 29, Elisabeth E. 8, Martha C. 8, Frances 6, Cora C. 4 (36)
SIMS, Caroline 36, Mary M. 15, Eli 8, Martha J. 43 (24)
SIMS, George H. 35, Louisa F. 37, Mary S. 12, Tennie F. 10, Nancy E. 8, William H. 7, Thomas A. 5, Robert J. 3, James A. 6/12 (33)
SIMS, James 12* (24)
SIMS, John 29* (43)
SINCLEAR, John 10* (B) (29)
SINCLEAR, Rebecca 40* (B), Tennie 4 (30)
SINGLETON, George W. 34, Martha C. 32, Maranda J. 8, Cintha E. 6, Lemuel W. 2 (31)
SINGLETON, James 28, Amanda C. 36, Lewis H. 12, Mary I. 8, John 6, William J.? 4, Ada S. 3, Mollie E. 4/21, Susannah 16, John W. 15 (32)
SINGLETON, James P. 36*, Sarah M. 33, Robert G. 11, James S. 6, Martha M. 3, Zebidee 5/12 (31)
SINGLETON, James W. 31, Elizabeth C. 26, Mary C. 8, Elmira A. 5, Dorcas G. 3, Christopher C. 1 (4)
SINGLETON, Martha 30*, John 1 (93)
SINGLETON, Willis O. 14* (32)
SKAGGS, Ann 17* (B), Cora 2, Fannie 7/12 (85)
SLATER, Cordelia 24* (13)

SLATER, James M. 32, Martha 27, John T. 8, George W. 5, Mary E. 11/12, John F. 21 (17)
SLATER, Sarah A. 31, Jane A. 13, Mary J. 1 (17)
SMALLEY, Mary J. 24* (17)
SMITH, A. H. 39 (m), Belle? 26, George J. C. 7, John W. 6, Pearl 4, Vesta 3, Anna 5/12, Emma 25 (87)
SMITH, Andy 20* (66)
SMITH, B. F. 44 (m)*, Betsey 38, Mary A. 14, Wm. 9, Sarah E. 3/12 (92)
SMITH, Betsy 45* (51)
SMITH, Calvin 21* (32)
SMITH, George W. jr. 24*, Isabel J. 22 (59)
SMITH, George W. sr. 57*, Jane 51, Andrew J. 22, Amanda? 16, Joseph E. 14, Robert E. 12, _____ 9 (f) (56)
SMITH, H. 43 (m), E. V. 32 (f), J. 16 (m), S. 10 (f), N. D. 7 (f), F. H. 5 (f), J. H. 3 (m), M. J. 1 (f) (72)
SMITH, Isaac 41, Mariah 44, Emily P. 16, Sarah T. 11 (22)
SMITH, J. R. 25 (m)*, A. J. 26 (f), J. R. 3 (m) (79)
SMITH, James A. 30, Mary E. 27, Rosana 7, Leora A. 5, John M. 1, Nancy 35 (8)
SMITH, John 29*, Sarah M. 24, Walter 4 (56)
SMITH, John C. 35, Elizabeth 29, William R. 10, Reuben 5, Sophia 3, Joseph 1 (22)
SMITH, John L. 8* (28)
SMITH, John W. 32*, Mary H? 37, Allice 10, Willie 8, Caldona 6, Sarah J. 4, Mary H. 10/12 (15)
SMITH, Joseph 47, Martha E. 40, Frances R. 18, Martha E. 17, Dove J. 13, Joseph 8, Omah 5, Oate 2 (11)
SMITH, K. C. 22 (f)* (48)
SMITH, Later? 26 (m)*, Eatha? A. 23, Dela 6, Jane 4 (92)
SMITH, Lou 10 (f)* (26)
SMITH, Louisa C. 33*, Armada E. 10 (24)
SMITH, Magie 10 (f)* (30)
SMITH, Martha 76* (85)
SMITH, Minerva J. 20*, William H. 17, Artela 14, Soosan C. 11 (35)
SMITH, Ruben 33*, Penelope E. 30, Emma M. 10, George E. 6, Cairie M. 4, Charles A. 2 (58)
SMITH, S. W. 47 (m), Tempy 41, S. M. 14 (f), M. A. 12 (f), E. G. 11 (m), M. L. 10 (f), Anderson 6, Detta 5 (66)
SMITH, W. G. 22 (m), M. 23 (f), W. P. 5/12 (m) (66)
SMOTHERS, Samuel 45, Ollie 56 (f), James 12, George 10, Samuel 7, William H. 2 (23)
SORRELS, John H. 14* (6)
SOUTHERLAND, Mill 23* (56)
SOUTHERLAND, T. J. 35 (m)*, J. B. 22 (m) (74)
SPARK, James 28 (B), Amanda C. 26, William L. 9, Samuel M. 7, James 4, Bryant 3, Mattie L. 11/12 (28)
SPARKS, Eliza 45*, Isaac 15 (17)
SPARKS, George 31, Martha A. 20, Elison 6/12 (26)
SPARKS, Jane 42* (B), Malinda 11, John 8, Cora 2 (19)
SPARKS, Patsy 27* (B), Andrew 2 (30)
SPARKS, Warren? 61* (B), Mary 49, Thomas 17 (26)
SPENCE, A. P. 30 (m), Sarah 30, Joseph 6, Wilford 4, Ila 2 (86)

SPENCE, C. P. 71? (m), Elizabeth 70, Providence 33 (90)
SPENCE, George 38*, Bettie 30, James 7, Richard E. 5, Sanford S. 3, Joseph E. 1, _____ 3/12 (m), James 12 (90)
SPENCE, J. T. 44 (m), M. E. 34 (f), M. J. 13 (f), Lizzie G. 7, Sallie A. 5, Wm. T. 2, Jack 1/12 (87)
SPENCE, Thomas 37, Eliza 25, John C. 7, James R. 5, Arch 2, _____ 1/12 (f) (91)
SPENCER, T. S.? 38 (m), Ella 25, T.? S. 5 (m), Marget 3, Joseph M. 2, Wm. R. 2/12, John L. 21 (85)
SPRANGER?, George 52 (B), Louisa 35, Mary 9, Charles W. [illegible], Edicor B. 7/12 (28)
SPRINGER, Aaron 39, Lavina 37 (25)
STAGNER, Onida? 71* (91)
STANFIELD, Isaac M. 42, Louisa C. 38, Lawrence B. 20, Isaac M. 15, Riley W. 14, Albert T. 10, Emmer C. 9, Dicus A. 7, John H. 4, Artia A. 2, unnamed 1/12 (f) (4)
STANFIELD, James 26, Maoma E. 16 (31)
STANFILL, John W. 29, Luiza C. 29, Joseph H. 7, Clemmy E. 4, Thomsa W. 3, Roxy A. 9/12 (4)
STANFILL, Thomas M. 55, Dillila 51, Amanda J. 17, Sary A. 12, Mary A. 10, Frances J. 3 (4)
STEAGAL, Josey 16* (58)
STEAGALD, Amanda 45* (55)
STEAGALD, Amanda 45* (B), Nancy 24, James 1 (55)
STEAGALD, Lucinda 38* (55)
STEARMAN, Martha 37, Martha E. 9 (25)
STEED, J. C. H. 42 (m)*, J. A. 30 (f), I. M. 1 (f) (81)
STEED, L. M. 75 (m), Sally 73, W. G. 51 (m), E. M. 40 (f), A. C. 30 (f), P. W. 27 (m), J. L. 17 (m), J. B. 15 (m) (84)
STEED, M. 35 (m), M. E. 24 (f) (79)
STEGALD, N. 31 (m)* (76)
STEPHENS, A. J. 23 (m)*, M. C. 17 (f) (83)
STEPHENS, Martha 26*, S. B. 3 (m), J. F. 2 (m) (74)
STEPHENS, William 65*, Tennessee 37, Joseph 12, Emma D. 3 (24)
STEPHENS, William L. 33, Elizabeth M. 18, Henry M. 3, Nathan T. 1 (25)
STEWARD, Washington G. 22* (26)
STEWARD, William A. 51, Sarah 35, Maybel M. 1, Mary A. 17, John W. 15 (29)
STIERS, Allen 64, Marie? 66 (88)
STILL, Geo. 58 (m), Jane 52, Kit 25 (m), Amanda 22, Brack 18, Dixie 14 (m), S. A. 11 (f), Jake 9 (71)
STILL, Leige 25*, J. 24 (f), E. M. 4 (f), V. 2 (f) (70)
STILLS, Marthy 54, M. 22 (f), A. 15 (m), A. M. 6/12 (f) (72)
STONE, Ephraim 45, Malind 39, Judea M. 5, Ephram L. 8/12 (1)
STOUT, Elijah 40 (B), Mira 49, Danl. M. 10, Alice M. 9, Cora C. 7 (44)
STOUT, John 22, Sallie W. 21, William R. 2/12 (56)
STOUT, William? 55*, Rosetta S. 35, Laura 20, Thomas 18, Cathaline 16, George 10, Oscar 10/12, Lile 33 (f) (B), Albert 12 (B) (57)
STRAYHORN?, Sarah J. 33* (56)
STREET, William F. 25, Mello? W. 26 (f), Anna M. 1 (56)
STRICKLIN, Catherine 35*, Mary E. 15, Reuben 8 (15)
STRICKLIN, J. T. 42 (m), Sary A. 38, Andrew J. 19, Frances A. 13, Roxy A. 10, Elizabeth R.

6, George L. 3, Franklin E. 4/12 (5)
STRICKLIN, John 75, Luticia E. 33 (6)
STRICKLIN, Peter 42, Susan M. 45, Lucy A. E. 13, William H. 8 (15)
STRICKLY, William H. 35, Pheriba E. 29, Jesse A. 12, William A. 6, Artela A. 4, Minor M. 1 (1)
STROCK, Jacob 35, Elizabeth 55, Mary E. 13, Hattie 9, Guilford J. 2 (24)
SUMMERSET, W. W. 62 (m), Rosanna 60 (92)
SWAFFORD, J. 21 (m)* (76)
SWAFFORD, J. L. 23 (m), M. G. 18 (f), A. E. 2/12 (f) (74)
SWAFFORD, M. A. 5 (f)*, L. F. 2 (f) (77)
SWINDLE, John W. 28, Rebeca 52 (12)
SWINDLE, William 22, Alabama 19, Frances V. 8/12 (17)
SWINN, Roathan? 19 (m)* (85)
SYKES, Jas. M. 27*, Sallie 25 (45)
SYKES, Zac 30, Jerusha 27, Sallie E. 5, Addi 2, Frances 1/12 (45)
TACKER, Bettie 35 (B), Hettie 13, Dee 9 (m), Ita 6, Isalone 4 (10)
TACKER, Frances A. 10* (B) (27)
TACKER, Iley 7 (m)* (8)
TALLEY, M. W. 45 (m), S. P. 42 (f), R. J. 19 (f), M. E. 17 (f), W. J. 15 (m), T. W. 13 (m), J. W. 11 (m), S. E. 7 (f) (76)
TAPLEY, James 18* (B) (21)
TARBET, Elijah E. 40*, Martha E. 28, Ida 6, Mary 4, Bertie 3 (f), Bessie 1 (31)
TATE, Francis A. 49, Louisa M. 43, Ann 18, Merady 14, Frank 11, Joseph 9, Betty 6 (54)
TATE, J. H. 21 (m), A. C. 18 (f) (49)
TATE, Jack 17, Vicy 16 (49)
TATE, James H. 23*, Emma 20, Jessee P. 3, Alla C. 2, ____ 11/365 (m) (56)
TATE, John L. 30, Martha J. 34, William H. 3, Carey B. 1, unnamed 1/12 (57)
TATE, Mattie 5* (55)
TATUM, Jesse B. 57, Harriet E. 48, Susan A. 26, John D. 24, Felix H. 19, Frances H. 17, Rober L. 15, Ittally O. 13, Ophelia F. 11, Jessee R. 7, Miles H. 22 (16)
TATUM, M. 21 (m)* (76)
TATUM, Robt. 19 (87)
TATUM, William 32, Elizabeth J. 25 (16)
TAYLOR, A. 33 (m), S. 32 (f), M. 8 (f), J. 6 (m), E. J. 3 (f), S. D. 1 (f) (72)
TAYLOR, A. J. 46 (m), Larthena 39, J. T. 18 (m), B. J. 16 (f), J. L. 14 (m), G. W. 13 (m), M. E. 11 (f), Martha 8, Arzara 6, V. A. 4 (f), E. A. 1 (f) (79)
TAYLOR, Albert 22*, John 21 (41)
TAYLOR, Benjamin 52, Frances C. 50, Fredonia C. 19, Benjamin 16, Rebecca E. 10, Hoy? W. J. 6 (m) (55)
TAYLOR, D. 25 (m)* (B) (69)
TAYLOR, H. B. 90 (m), V. 25 (f), M. A. 6 (f), W. H. 3 (m) (70)
TAYLOR, J. W. 28 (m), M. M. 26 (f), J. C. 9 (m), J. A. 7 (m), W. B. T. 5 (m), S. L. 2 (m), G. W. 4/2 (m) (68)
TAYLOR, Jas. E. 41, M. E. 38 (f), John H. 18, M. J. 16 (f), E. A. 14 (f), S. B. 10 (f), G. L. 8 (m), M. F. 5 (f), B. A. 2 (f), O. E. 4/12 (f) (46)
TAYLOR, John 11* (B) (28)
TAYLOR, John 70, V. A. 67? (f) (71)
TAYLOR, Louis 60*, Saba 60, Adaline 21, Hardee 17, Ely 28, Mary 18 (93)

TAYLOR, Lyda 32* (B), George A. 10 (21)
TAYLOR, Rebeca M. 47, Jane 46 (6)
TAYLOR, S. K. 47 (m), R. J. 39? (f), J. W. 18 (m), J. P. 16 (m), M. C. 14 (f), S. C. 12 (f), S. J. 8? (f), L. J. 4 (f), S. W. 7 (m), S. J.? 1 (f) (68)
TAYLOR, William 18* (19)
TEAGUE, John 16* (51)
TEAGUE, M. R. 48 (m)*, M. J. 28 (f), M. S. 20 (f) (74)
TEAGUE, Winey E. 38, William H. 11, Jesse C. 7, Rosetta 1 (6)
TEBBS, Unisa? 87*, Jane 54, U. 30 (f), L. 25 (f), S. A. F. 4 (f), unnamed 1/12 (f), H. P. 3 (m) (66)
TEEBLES, G. A. 46 (m), S. A. 44 (f), J. A. 20 (m), J. C. 17 (m), M. E. 15 (f), H. J. 11 (m), A. 10 (m), M. 6 (f), A. B. 4 (f) (63)
TERRY, Julie H. 16* (90)
TERRY, N. A. 37 (m), Susan E. 34, Elizabeth 10, Lucy B. 7, Dora Bell 5, Mary A. 4, Samuel S. 2, Woodly J. 1 (86)
TERRY?, Wm. 41, Martha 34, Kibby? 13 (m), John 8 (88)
THARP, William 19* (16)
THOMAS, J. H. 43 (m), Mary 38, L. B. 15 (f), E. 12 (f), J. L. 7 (m) (66)
THOMAS, J. H. 48 (m)*, R. J. 33 (f), A. B. 16 (m), M. D. 13 (m), N. L. 9 (m), G. H. 3 (m), K. 4/12 (m) (75)
THOMAS, J. S. 28 (m), S. R.? 18 (f) (66)
THOMAS, John H. 51*, Mary E. 37, Maggy 12, Martha J. 11, Thomas A. 8, Jacob R. 7 (36)
THOMAS, Seth 42*, E. C. 43 (f), A. T. 10 (m), M. D. 9 (f), E. B. 3 (m), A. D. 2 (m), W. C. 32 (m), S. J. 47 (f) (66)
THOMPSON, A. 64 (f)* (81)
THOMPSON, A.? F. 41 (m), Artha M. 39 (f), James 15, Ada J. 13, Francis 13, David A. 11, R. D. 9 (m), Mary W. 6, Martha A. 3, Willis C. 1/12 (92)
THOMPSON, Mary J. 13* (3)
THOMPSON, Robert 23* (32)
THOMPSON, S. 28 (f)*, J. M. L. 6/12 (f) (78)
THOMPSON, Thomas 52, Sarah A. 50, John W. 12, Nancy? J. 10, Anna B. 4 (51)
THOMPSON, W. M. 47 (m), P. R. 38 (f), U. E. 20 (f), W. B. 19 (m), M. A. 15 (f), H. E. 12 (f), J. A. 11 (f), G. A. 11 (f), O. J. 8 (f), J. J. 6 (m) (81)
THOMPSON, Wm. H. 19* (52)
THORNTON, George 35, Arta M. 33, Norar S. 14, Aradelle 12, Sallie 7, Katie 5, Vida 3, Ethel 1, E. J. 65 (f) (88)
THORNTON, Lucinda 42*, Manora? 21, John T. 14 (90)
THORNTON, Thos. 37, Eleza 28, Etta 12, Lizzie 7, Annie? 5, Becie 3, Robert 1 (88)
THREAT, James 20* (39)
THREAT, Paten L. 28*, Harrett 17, Albert L. 1 (36)
TIBBS, Monroe 21, Dora 23, A. 2/12 (f) (65)
TICE, Mathew 17*, Dean 15 (20)
TIDWELL, Eliza 50* (25)
TIDWELL, William J. 40, Matilda C. 42, Cintha J. 18, Martha M. 15, Robert J. 12, Samuel V. 10, Mary J. 7, Margaret E. 5, Virgo V. 2 (9)
TILLMAN, Elisabeth 50?*, William 28, Fraces 21 (39)
TILMAN, Hugh 24, Laury 24 (39)
TISHER, Dudley 16* (B) (21)

TOLE, George 40 (B), Harett 25, Fanny 8, Norah 5, Jefferson 3, Nancy 1 (35)
TOLL, Elizabeth 57, Eliza J. 23 (24)
TOLLY, Arther 52, Mary 41, James A. 21, Martin A. 18, Joseph T. 13, John A. 10, Samuel J. 8, Dossy A. 13, Mary E. 1 (41)
TOLLY, George 26, Rebecca 19 (38)
TOLLY, Joseph 57* (38)
TOWNSELL, G. 29 (m)* (B), A. 28 (f), H. 10 (m), S. 9 (f), John 7, W. 5 (m), A. D. 1 (m) (74)
TRIPLET, Elizabeth 35, C. L. 22 (f), S. A. 20 (f), M. A. 18 (f), E. H. 16 (f), W. A. 14 (f), L. T. 12 (m), L. B. 10 (f), Jno. W. 4 (49)
TUBBS, J. W. 35 (m), Elizabeth 35, Mattie F. 7, Harvey L. 4, Franky 2, Sallie A. 1 (47)
TUBBS, L.? C. 46 (m), Gambo 44 (f), Aurora S. 20, Richard 13, George 11 (89)
TUBBS, R. 46 (m), M. C. 39 (f), W. G. 17 (m), S. 14 (f), M. E. 5 (f), E. E. 3 (m), S. S. 1 (m) (71)
TUBBS, S. Jack 52*, Cris K. A. 21 (f), A. Washington 13, C. Ann 11 (46)
TUBBS, Sarilda 15* (85)
TUBBS, T. P. 23 (m)*, Liza 30, D. D. 10/12 (m) (63)
TUCK, Philip E. 34*, Martha 24, William E. 4, Charles 2 (42)
TUCK, William H. 33*, Emily J. 22, Maude E. 1, Albert N. 5/12, Jennie G. 9, Jackson 2 (57)
TUCKER, Alexander 38, Mary J. 41, Amanda J. 13, Frances A. 11, George J. 10, Sarah E. 7, Racheal L. 4, John A. 2 (16)
TUCKER, Alexander L. 24, Malinda C. 20, James W. 7/12 (17)
TUCKER, Andrus J. 24 (10)
TUCKER, G. F. 25 (m), N. E. 31 (f), Sarah E. 5, Mitchel A. 1 (54)
TUCKER, George H.? 23, Lucinda A. 19 (5)
TUCKER, George W. 79 (13)
TUCKER, James J. 54, Sarah J. 51, Permelia A. 30, Emily E. 18, Carroll V. 17, Leonard T. B. 15 (12)
TUCKER, James M. 21, Safrona J. 14 (12)
TUCKER, Jefferson D. 18, Mary L. 28 (12)
TUCKER, John A. 30, Sarah V. 30, Lucy 9, Nancy P? 1 (15)
TUCKER, John F. 28, Frances E. 32, William T. 7, John C. 5, George C. 3, Jerry D. 1 (13)
TUCKER, John I.? 20, Emily T. 21 (58)
TUCKER, John W. 48*, Martha J. 41, Benard A. 18, Sarah E. 14, Mary A. 12, Estelee 10, Catherine 8, John N. S. 6, Margaret J. 4 (13)
TUCKER, Newton G. 58*, Nancy J. 56, Thomas A. 28, Mary A. 32, Mary J. P. 6, Kitrila A. P. 5, Newton A. 4, Lavica 2 (20)
TUCKER, R. Houston 34, Sarah B. 25, William D. 7, John M. 5, Mary A. 4, Rosannah 1, James W. 3/12 (9)
TUCKER, Solomon 40, Martha A. 30, Rosillar P. 10, John L. 6, Medora E. 5, Mary K. 4, Frances E. 5/12 (16)
TUCKER?, Sarah E. 8* (29)
TULL, James 37* (B), Mary 42, Mary 13, Allen 10, Cora 7 (28)
TURNBO, Harriet 50* (17)
TURNBO, Jane 38*, Sarah 12, John W. 10, William U. 7 (19)
TURNBO, Nathan 66*, Elizabeth 44, Allice B. 17, Nannie V. 14, William N. 12, Mary E. 10, Fannie L. 6 (19)
TURNBO, Widow 43* (11)

TURNER, James M. 45, Mary Jane 37, Matty 18, Henry J. 17, Elisabeth 14, William J. 13, Leonard 12, Joseph 11, Dorah 7, Benjamin F. 5, George W. 4, Charles 10, Albert 9/12 (34)
TURNER, James W. 5* (19)
TURNER, William A. 37, Margarett M. 29, John G. 12, Margarett C. 9, Thos. F. 7, Mary E. 3, Jessee L. 1 (19)
TURPEN, Wm. 5* (88)
TUTEN, G. W. 52 (m)*, Mary 46, John F. 19, L. Arabel 16, Wm. J. 14, M. Ellen 12, N. Anna 10, F. Catherine 2 (50)
TUTEN, John I. 31, Frances J. 20, Ora 1, Ida Bell 1/12 (27)
TUTEN, Wiliam R. 30*, Nancy E. 26, William F. 5, Sarah H. 3, Clauda R. 2 (m) (27)
TUTON, John W. 24, Martha J. 22, Mary E. 5, Eller J. 2 (14)
TUTON?, Julia A. 54, James R. 20, George W. 18, Arrilla J. 30 (12)
TYLER, J. I. 24 (m), M. 21 (f), C. J. 5 (f), C. 1 (m) (84)
TYLER, T. J. 32 (m), N. C. 38 (f), A. 19 (f), J. W. 12 (m), M. E. 11 (f), T. L. 8 (m), J. M. 6 (m), L. 4 (f), E. W. 2 (m) (76)
TYNER, Littleton 25, Mary E. 19, Dorah D. 2, Flora T. 5/12 (22)
VANDINE, M. 54 (m)*, H. 41 (f), M. 71 (f), L. 8/12 (f) (73)
VAUGHN, D. 13 (m)* (B) (64)
VEAL, Henry 38, Eliza J. 36, Z. E. 10 (f), M. P. 6 (f), Jessee W. 4, John 2 (45)
VEAL, J. P. 46 (m), Sophronia 34, Mary 4, Jessie 2, Infant 1/12 (f) (74)
VEAL, M. 70 (m)*, M. P. 48 (f), Jackson 20 (77)
VEAL, M. F. 16 (f)* (44)
VICTORY, Joseph 16* (B) (19)
VOCE, William 29, Mary E. 22 (34)
VOCE?, George H. 53, Tennessee 47, George M. 16, Eli 14, Little 11, Virgie 6 (34)
VOLNER, Francis M. 47, Susannah 40, Susannah 13, Artelia 10, Phillip S. 8, Francis M. 6, William T. 4, Cintha A. 1 (6)
VOLNER, James J. 265, Safrona A. 21, James F. 4, Starling C. 2, Mary L. 4/12 (3)
VOLNER, John F. 23 (3)
VOLNER, Josephus E. 21, Eliza J. 22, Monroe 1 (3)
VOSS, James 30, Sarah B. 21, Emma 3, William A. 9/12 (36)
WADE, Charles E. 65, Nancy A. M. 43, Riley L. 10, Martin A. 8, Nancy E. J. 5, Martha F. 3 (15)
WAFFORD, S. 6 (m)* (63)
WALACE, Dixon 43, Lucresa E. 37, Walace 8, Sally 1 (38)
WALACE, Easter 18* (B) (38)
WALACE, Ellen 21 (B), Victora 3, Mamy 11/12 (41)
WALACE, John T. 31, Sarah 11, Rodela 5, Harrett T. 50 (39)
WALACE, Samuel M. 30*, Emely E. 28, Sarah E. 3 (39)
WALACE, Tennessee 23* (B) (38)
WALACE, Tennessee 23* (B) (40)
WALACE, William M. 29*, Mary J. 28, Walter W. 5, Joseph S. 3 (39)
WALDON, Thomas 26*, Rachel? 19, Freddie 1 (93)
WALKER, A. 35 (m)* (B), C. 22 (f), A. 6 (f), B. 4 (f), D. 2 (f) (73)
WALKER, Arthena 11*, Pollie 73 (87)
WALKER, Charlott 76* (93)
WALKER, Geo. 52* (B), Mary 32, Wm. 17, Hiram 14, Sarah 12, A. 8 (m), L. S. 3 (f), Sam

7/12 (63)

WALKER, George W. 40*, Rebecca 36 (20)

WALKER, H. C. 41 (m)*, Janette 39, Eddie 13, Bittie 10, Dora 5, Wm. H. 3 (87)

WALKER, J. S. 56 (m), Emeline 25, Frankey 19 (f), Valreah 17, Mattie 14, Wm. 8, Leonia 6, Lillie 3 (87)

WALKER, J. T. 36 (m), Mary 36, L. S. 17 (m), C. M. 13 (f), P. N. 11 (m), M. A. 8 (f), M. T. 8 (m), Ida A. 7, S. A. 5 (f), J. T. 3 (m), unnamed 5/12 (f) (61)

WALKER, J. W. 10 (m)*, D. R. 7 (m) (75)

WALKER, J. W. 80 (m)* (61)

WALKER, James 51 (B), Bell 30, Samuel 18, Jinny 10, Henry 14, Helsard 11, Mary 7, Fabny 6 (f), James jr. 5, Hannah 2 (35)

WALKER, Jane 50* (B), Samuel 15, Amos 12, Robert 8 (34)

WALKER, Jeremiah 53, Malinda A. 39, Mary A. 15, John 12, James 10, Rebecca 4, Kitty 1 (20)

WALKER, MaLINDA 17* (B) (23)

WALKER, Nancy 70 (B), Hannah 17, David 13, Linda 14, Darah 12 (35)

WALKER, O. A. 26 (m), Mary F. 16, Blanch 1 (87)

WALKER, Orlena M. 35, Ulysis G. 15, Armetta 10, John B. 4 (20)

WALKER, Peter 29 (B), Ellen 5, William 1/12 (17)

WALKER, Rosa 40 (B), Charley 15, Will 13, John 7, Lucy 10, Harriett 5 (35)

WALKER, Serilda 43, William 21, George 15, Garrett 14, Ollie 10 (f) (25)

WALKER, Stephen 70 (B), Hannah 50, Reuben 12, Carroll 10, Alfred 6 (35)

WALL, W. W. 27 (m), L. F. 24 (f), L. C. 2 (f) (44)

WALLACE, B. 70 (m) (B), Rose 61, Lisie 13 (81)

WALLACE, B. 72 (f), J. W. 18 (m), W. 14 (f) (82)

WALLACE, Bert 23* (B) (27)

WALLACE, Darthona 16* (B) (42)

WALLACE, J. M. 46 (m)*, Elisabeth 44, Mary 10, S. G. 5 (m) (82)

WALLACE, James A. 17* (B) (42)

WALLACE, M. 35 (m), S. 26 (f), W. 12 (m), J. 10 (m), T. 8 (m), L. 6 (f), A. 4 (f), B. 1 (f) (72)

WALLACE, S. G. 44 (m), M. A. 38 (f), L. A. 15 (f), W. W. 12 (m), R. A. 9 (f), C. F. 4 (f) (79)

WALLER, Wiley F. 26, Sarah E. 21 (20)

WALLS, H. H. 42 (f)*, M. E. 15 (f) (74)

WALTERS, George 6* (57)

WALTERS, George W. 44*, Elizabeth E. 38, John 20, George A. 15, Lula 13, Charles 7 (58)

WALTERS, William A. 42, Fredona T. 19, George W. 6, Andrewson D. 2, Margurite A. 8/12 (40)

WARD, A. J. 43 (m), A. M. 36 (f), A. O. 16 (f), A. L. 13 (m), E. J. 12 (m), Emma 9, M. 2 (m), unnamed 11/12 (f) (64)

WARDEN, Saml. C. 45*, C. N.? C. 21 (f), H. A. 20 (m), L. A. 12 (f) (51)

WARDEN, William 26, Laverna 22?, Samuel F. 4, John T. 1 (56)

WARFIELD, Eliza 28 (34)

WARNER, Frank 24*, Nancy 23, Wm. F. 1 (93)

WARREN, Alzada 45, William 17, Caroline 13, Thomas 22 (38)

WARREN, James J. 38*, Huldah E. 28, Sarah E. 5 (30)

WARREN, John J. 30, Margaret E. 20, Starlin G. 3, Daniel K.? 1 (5)

WATSON, A. 14 (m)* (63)
WATSON, A. 63 (m)*, Pheba 53 (80)
WATSON, Clint 24, Marthy 35, J. H. 2 (m) (62)
WATSON, J. 59 (m), Mary 47, Wm. 18, James 13, Florence 9 (65)
WATSON, J. F. 21 (m)* (44)
WATSON, N. 22 (m), Sarah 15, L. B. 3/12 (m) (75)
WATSON, Simon P. 52, Zilpha 42, Martha J. 8, Zilpha A. 6, Nora A. 3 (31)
WATSON, W. T. 28 (m), J. A. 21 (f) (44)
WAYDLE?, William M. 15* (6)
WEAVER, George W. 49, Elisabeth 42, Samuel 17, Eliza 15, William H. 13, Franklin 11, Mary E. 2 (36)
WEBB, Henry 43, Marget 34, Henry A. 15, Rosan 17, Jane F. 13, Iserel 11, Fedora 10/12 (92)
WEBB, Wm. 31, Mary J. 31, Lily B. 6, Silas J. 2 (92)
WELCH, David 56*, Harriett 49, Leonard 20, George 18, Nicholas 13 (55)
WELCH, Elijah 45*, Martha R. 42, Joannah 20, Rose 20, William 18, Fredonia 15 (53)
WELCH, Henry 58*, Mary 54, Reuben N. 24, Nancy B. 17, Patrick H. 14, Cadwell? J. 24 (55)
WELCH, Isiah 43*, Winny 41, G. F. 23 (f), A. J. 14 (f), Henry 6, J. J. 2 (f) (45)
WELCH, Jerry 50, F. E. 47 (f), E. M. 21 (f), R. N. 18 (m), F. L. 13 (m), M. N. 8 (f), F. F. 5 (f) (45)
WELCH, John L. 24, Rebecca 24, Emily 6, Maggie 4, Fielding 2 (55)
WELCH, Margurett 8* (B) (25)
WELCH?, Elis 35, Florinda 34, Mollie 13, Bell 9, George 10/12 (88)
WELLS, Arthur D. 23, Jane 29 (26)
WELLS, Elener S. 63* (8)
WELLS, Eliza 26*, Ewing 1 (24)
WESBROOK, J. W. 19 (m)* (75)
WESSON, Minnie 45* (51)
WESSON, Sarah 47*, Robert 19, Mollie 16, Ella 14, Dick 13, Stone W. 12, Joseph E. 8, Jinnie 5 (88)
WEST, Benjamin W. 20* (21)
WEST, S. Penelton 32(f), O. Mary 13, James I. 11, William W. 9, Fred E. 4, Saml. D. C. 2 (43)
WEST, Sallie 24* (B) (21)
WESTERN, L. 45 (f), Riley 10 (63)
WESTERN, Mary 28*, Eliza J. 10, Wilson 8, Catherine 6 (46)
WESTON, David 50*, Charity J. 48, William C. 17, Robert P. 13, Charity J. jr. 12, Sophia E. 5 (30)
WESTON, James Z. 24*, Sophrona 22, Lura E. 1 (29)
WETHERFORD, Robert E. 65, Elizabeth 39, Dora 11, Susan G. 8, Josie E. 6, James K. 4 (17)
WHEELER, Mary 77* (7)
WHITAKER, Houston 18* (B) (21)
WHITE, A. 21 (m)* (B) (74)
WHITE, Alex 24 (B), Middy 15, Chaney 80 (f) (59)
WHITE, Alfred 38* (B), Easter 25, George 6 (38)
WHITE, Alpa O. 12*, Mary B. 10, Lee W. 7 (53)

WHITE, Americus L. 25, Mary E. 16 (3)
WHITE, C. H. W. 38 (m), Martha E. 29, Willie E. 1 (f) (28)
WHITE, Cornelius F. 28, Nicy J. 25, Geo. W. 5, Lee W. 3, Cornelius P. 10 (52)
WHITE, Daniel 45 (B), Chaney 21 (f), Frank 14, Maggie 12, Amanda A. 11, Zac 4?, Elizabeth 4, Nathaniel 3 (53)
WHITE, David 22* (B), Easter 24, Eliza A. 1, William 5/12, Ann 53, Aaron 17 (28)
WHITE, Felix 18* (B) (53)
WHITE, George 24, Adaline? 26 (54)
WHITE, George W. 35* (24)
WHITE, Harvey 38 (B), Silva 30, Louisa 18, Thomaas 12, Henrietta 5, Willis 3/12 (54)
WHITE, Henry 53, Mary J. 46, Frances 19, James H. 15, Mary Allice 8, George W. 4 (32)
WHITE, Isaac L. 30, Nancy E. 69 (16)
WHITE, Isaih F. 33, Nancy C. 22, Felix F. 10, Ida 7, Estellee 4, Tiney 2 (17)
WHITE, Jemima 67 (53)
WHITE, Joanna 49, George 18, Charles J. 16, Harvy F. 12 (2)
WHITE, John H. 40*, Manda 33, Mary L. 7, Eliza E. 4, John L. 3 (13)
WHITE, Loney 35 (B), Elizabeth 25, James F. 2 (53)
WHITE, Marion 21 (m)* (53)
WHITE, Milly 30 (B), Emily 17, Martha 13, William H. 9, James A. 4 (4)
WHITE, N. 27 (f)* (B) (74)
WHITE, N. D. 59 (m), Calhoun 29, Serathena 19, Mills 19, Hannah 72 (54)
WHITE, Nowel 60*, Nancy J. 35, Charles 19, William 16, Susan 13 (57)
WHITE, Paralee 45* (52)
WHITE, Philip 24* (B) (56)
WHITE, R. Alexander 23, Frances S. 23, C. E. 1 (m), Harvey 22 (B) (53)
WHITE, R. Altus 46 (m)*, E. J. 42 (f), Thos. A. 16, R. W. 13 (m), Nick 6, Geo. F. 2 (51)
WHITE, Ransom 70 (B), Charity 45, Hannah 22, Ellen 6, William 3, Lucy 9/12 (55)
WHITE, Rebecca 83* (19)
WHITE, Riley 34* (B), Mary F. 29, Alace 15, Ida 11, Alex 6, Fanny 3, ____ 5/365 (m) (53)
WHITE, T. R. 34 (m)*, E. J. 33 (f), J. W. 7 (m), N. E. 2 (f), Lusinda 54, James 20 (61)
WHITE, Uphrey 46*, Martha A. 45, William 19, Mary E. 15, Sarah A. 14, Leslie T. 12, Nancy E. 10 (32)
WHITE, Wiley 53*, Rebecca 52 (52)
WHITE, William 21* (B) (56)
WHITE, William 48, Delilah 31, James R. 8, John T. 6, Martha J. 3, Mary E. 5/12, Louisa 54, Francis M. 16 (24)
WHITE, William A. 24, Amanda E. 19 (3)
WHITE, Zac 52, Louisa J. 45, John H. 18, Martha E. 17, Nancy J. 16, Robert L. 13, Ruben 10, William 5 (59)
WHITE?, Marshal 24, Lucinda 20, Sally A. 3 (9)
WHITTAKER, John 7* (B) (16)
WHOLESONVER?, Elizabeth 63* (24)
WILEY, John W. 31, Allice 25, Robert L. 2 (9)
WILEY, Mary F. 24 (9)
WILKINS, F. P. 27 (m)*, M. S. 33 (f), Cora B. 4/12 (61)
WILKINS, Osker K. 1* (31)
WILKINS, W. A. 37 (m), R. A. 34 (f), J. W. 13 (m), W. A.? 10 (m), J. M. 9 (m), H. P. 7 (m), Ezral 5, M. B. 2 (f), Mary A. R.? 10/12 (81)

WILKINS, Wm. A. 61, A. C. 52 (f), Alfonzo 19? (60)
WILLIAMS, A. 26 (m) (B), M. 29 (f), D. W. 10 (m), S. F. 8 (f), J. H. 6 (m), N. A. 5 (f), M. B. 3? (f), Emmer 3/12? (77)
WILLIAMS, D. 11 (m)* (B) (71)
WILLIAMS, D. E. 40 (m)*, Lucy 40, George? 18, Jennie 11, Mattie 7 (86)
WILLIAMS, Dorah 19* (33)
WILLIAMS, Elizabeth 75* (85)
WILLIAMS, Frank 35* (B), Esther 23, Franklin 15 (17)
WILLIAMS, J. B. 68 (m)* (74)
WILLIAMS, John 30, Mary 28, James 9, Eddie 6, _____ 4/12 (m) (85)
WILLIAMS, Lavina 63, M. E. 26 (f) (49)
WILLIAMS, N. N. 45 (m), F. C. 38 (f), W. J. 21 (m), O. W. 16 (m), J. H. 13 (m), E. J. 10 (f), Granvill 8, M. L. 6 (f), C. M. 2 (f), ____ 2/12 (f) (49)
WILLIAMS, Robert 55* (B), Moses 25, Chany 12 (f), Lousia 21 (29)
WILLIAMS, W. E. 19 (m), N. A. 19 (f), Noah 10/12 (50)
WILLITS, Walter J. 17* (90)
WILLS, E. 37 (f), Elie 18 (m), L. 14 (f) (69)
WILSON, Elisabeth 66 (34)
WILSON, Hiram H. 50, Nancy J. 41, Mary F. 25, William L. 22, John M. 19, Joseph B. 16, Florence P. 14, Thomas R. 11, Eudora A. 10, Laura J. 6, Anna L. 1 (20)
WILSON, Hiram W. 33, Elizabeth 28, Edward 9, John 6, Minnie 4, William 2 (23)
WILSON, Isaac 20, Nancy 21, John G. 1 (34)
WILSON, James 26, Nannie 25, John F. 3, Sam 1, James 54, Martha M. 17 (88)
WILSON, James 28* (19)
WILSON, James M. 47, Martha E. 28, William M. 16, Samuel H. 13, Nannie I? 11, Mary E. 9, Jinnie L. A. 7, John W. 40 (20)
WILSON, John 48 (34)
WILSON, Manley H. 28, Sarah 27, Enily 2, Lilly 9/12, Z. Forrest 19 (10)
WILSON, Mary 100* (61)
WINCHESTER, James M. 35, Mary J. 37, Eliza A. R. 7, James F. 3 (5)
WINCHESTER, Mary 60* (2)
WINES, Marthy 21* (61)
WINES, Sarah 62, J. W. 22 (m) (61)
WINTERS, J. C. 33 (m), Frances 33, J. 12 (f), S. 6 (f), R. 3 (m), Wm. 1 (66)
WISE, John D. 31*, S. A. 44 (f), E. E. 4 (f) (60)
WISE, M. A. 54 (f)*, M. J. 21 (f), M. F. 19 (f), S. E. 16 (f), M. M. J. 13 (f), J. W. 2 (m) (82)
WOOD, Edgar 22*, Larcena 19, Elvena 9/12, Ruthee 65, Harriet 45 (93)
WOOD, George 19* (87)
WOOD, George 26, Julia M. 20, Lewis? A. 2, Mary E. 1 (91)
WOOD, George 75, Enal? 68 (f), Laura 45 (93)
WOOD, J. F. 44 (m)*, M. A. 43 (f) (61)
WOOD, John K. 59, Nancy B. 53, Edwin H. 17, Mary E. 15, Cora 11 (92)
WOOD, L. L. 31 (m), W. M. 23 (f) (64)
WOOD, Theodore 30*, Marget M. 24, Cora V. 3, _____ 5/12 (m) (92)
WOODARD, H. G. 58 (m)*, E. 59 (f), M. G. 16 (f) (65)
WOODS, C. W. 36 (f), S.? B. 15 (f), J. E. 13 (m), H. L. 9 (m). M. M. 6 (m), G. A. 3 (m), Thomas 10/12 (81)
WOODS, Eveline 45 (B), William 13, Martha 5 (42)

WOODS, M. 30 (m), S. C. 39 (f), M. J. 9 (f), J. M. 8 (m), F. M. 6 (m), J. V. 4 (m), J. J. 1 (m) (84)
WOODS, Parlie 41* (88)
WOODS, R. P. 52 (m), Loise J. 40 (f), Margaret 13, Franklin 11, Kendric 8, Frances 5 (92)
WRIGHT, E. B. 23 (m), Martha 21, Henry L. 4/12, Saml. C. 9 (54)
WRIGHT, Eddy 25, M. Jane 24, Charles 1 (49)
WRIGHT, John 67, Mary 60, H. J. 37 (m) (54)
WRIGHT, John 8* (22)
WRIGHT, Lemuel S. 34*, Amand 27, Aida L. 2 (24)
WRIGHT, Martha 50, Zucarilla 22 (m) (24)
WRIGHT, Martha 62 (22)
WRIGHT, William B. 38, Margarett 34, Mary E. 7, John H. 4 (26)
WRIGHT, Wm. M. 39, A. Amanda 44, J. Noland 9, A. May 8, W. Thomas 6 (49)
WYATT, Elisha 64, Mahalia 58, Sarah A. 30, Martha J. 27, Clarkee C. 25, Mary C. 17, John 32, James R. 8, Mary C. 6, Kinchen A. 2 (9)
WYATT, George M. 45, Nancy J. 44, Thomas J. 18, William D. 15, Nancy J. 14, James F. 11, Enely T. 1, General J. 3, Syntha P. 6 (36)
WYATT, George W. 30, Florence 22, Minnie L. 6/12 (9)
WYATT, James R. 46*, Elvira 49, Wesley A. 19, David C. 17, Sarah A. 14, John F. 12, Alfred R. 10, Eugene A. 6, Mary 83 (33)
WYATT, Jessee 48, Nancy E. 35, Mahalia E. 17, Sary J. 13, Mally 3 (f), Margarett 1, James K. 8 (10)
WYATT, John 20* (32)
WYATT, Millard F. 22, Emily B. 21, William H. 6/12 (24)
WYATT, Richard 23*, Verdeline 18, Daniel W. 1, Joseph E. 28 (41)
WYATT, Robert H. 23, Louisa E. 25, Ann E. 1 (9)
WYATT, Samuel 33*, Mary E. 32, Ellen 13, Levi W. 7, Sallie 2 (28)
WYATT, William D. 62, Isabell E. 61, Mary F. 31, William 21, Margurite 19, Betty 17 (41)
YARBRO, Aaron 68* (B), Ellen 48, Ann 25 (56)
YARBRO, Allen 39 (B), Malinda 53, Margarett 72, Celia 38, Sam 34, Myra 18, Elizabeth 9, Arrena 7, C. E. 2/12 (m) (19)
YARBRO, Amanda J. 52* (58)
YARBRO, Ann Eliza 37, Jennie 16, Laura 11, George 9, Arretta 7, Dorah E. 2 (24)
YARBRO, Anna 21* (B), Orra 8/12 (25)
YARBRO, Bob 29 (B), Ann 24, Vena A. 8, Eve A. 7, Lucy A. 3, Perry W. 8/12 (36)
YARBRO, Carr 24 (B), Henrietta 24, Ella 4, Ernest 3, Asale 1 (f), Ules 1/12 (42)
YARBRO, Charlie E. C. 24, Mary E. 23, John W. 3, William H. 1 (36)
YARBRO, Dafney 70 (B) (11)
YARBRO, Daniel 25* (B), Esther 19, Willie 1 (16)
YARBRO, Delilah 72*, John L. 34, Sarah 19, Martha J. 44, Nancy E. 38, Jos. 27, Linsey S. 2, Lorenza D. 32 (19)
YARBRO, Dink? 14 (m)* (B) (57)
YARBRO, George 36* (24)
YARBRO, James A. 21, Ann 18 (23)
YARBRO, Joe 21 (B), Malinda 20, Lucy 8/12 (11)
YARBRO, John 39 (B), Lovie 33, Eliza J. 12, James 10, Joseph 9, Martha A. 7, John 3 (23)
YARBRO, John T. 40*, Elisabeth M. 35, Hery M. 18, Mary A. 15, Thomas C. 13, Cora M. 4, William T. 1 (36)

YARBRO, Joseph F. 49, Sarah J. 31, Dorah A. 3, Mary N. 1, William J. 3/12 (25)
YARBRO, Joseph G. 50*, Mary A. 40, Jacob F. 21, Mary E. 16, Robt. E. 14, Sophra 11, Michal 7 (22)
YARBRO, Judy E. 60*, Caty 40 (B), Peter 16 (B), Charlott 28 (B), James 8 (B) (36)
YARBRO, Martha 43, Martha A. 16? (23)
YARBRO, Mary A. 50* (B) (19)
YARBRO, Milton J. 48, Minerva 42, Mary V. 17, Martha A. 15, William H. 11, John T. 9, Allice D. 7, Edmund 5, John 14 (B) (25)
YARBRO, Rebecca 30* (B), James 9, Martha 7, Magaline 3 (42)
YARBRO, Rhoda 33 (B), Robert 9, Henry W. 5, W. R. 3 (m) (51)
YARBRO, Rufus M. 37, Susan E. 25, Nancy 6, Benjamin D. 4, Alminda 1 (22)
YARBRO, Wade 22* (B), Charity 17, Eddy 2/12, G. A. 14 (f) (19)
YARBRO, William E. 25, Nancy 24, Cecil 2 (m), Zeneda 1/12 (m) (58)
YARBROL, Jef 25* (B), Ollie 31 (f), Bettie 5, Daniel 1 (30)
YOUNG, Emit 17* (B) (52)
YOUNG, John B. 34, Mary R. 33, Emely A. 10, James F. 9, Dorah E. 5, Nancy E. 5/12 (37)
YOUNG, John R. 30, Sophrona C. 25, James W. 9, Charles M. 7, Robert P. 2 (8)
YOUNG, Louisa 6* (38)
YOUNG, Penelope 48, Elenora J. 20, R. Thurston 18, S. Valdale 16, F. Clayton 13, A. B. 7 (f) (43)
YOUNG, Robert M. 42, Mary Jane 41, Sarah E. 21, John B. 18, Mary E. 16, Joseph Ann 13, Syren J. 10 (m), Adam 6, Dula 2 (38)
YOUNG, William D. 46*, Catharine 47, Isaac M. 15, William H. H. 12 (41)
YOUNG, Zack T. 31*, Soosan C. 37, James M. 5 (38)
YOURY, William F. 21*, Sarah F. 19, Willis 2 (58)
ZARBRO, Lee 16 (m)* (B) (52)

www.ingramcontent.com/pod-product-compliance
Lightning Source LLC
LaVergne TN
LVHW010543100826
845148LV00013B/2588
9781596411142